Between Talk and Teaching

Between Talk and Teaching

Reconsidering the Writing Conference

LAUREL JOHNSON BLACK
Indiana University of Pennsylvania

UTAH STATE UNIVERSITY PRESS
Logan, Utah
1998

Utah State University Press
Logan, Utah 84322-7800
© Copyright 1998 Utah State University Press.
All rights reserved.

Typography by WolfPack

Manufactured in the United States of America.
98 99 00 01 02   5 4 3 2 1

Library of Congress Cataloging-in-Publication Data
Black, Laurel Johnson, 1957-
    Between talk and teaching : reconsidering the writing conference /
Laurel Johnson Black.
       p. cm.
    Includes bibliographical references.
    ISBN 0-87421-241-3
    1. English language--Rhetoric--Study and teaching. 2. Report
writing--Study and teaching (Higher) 3. Teacher-student
relationships. 4. Tutors and tutoring. I. Title.
PE1404.B587 1998
808'.042'07--dc21   97-45436
                                                    CIP

I would like to thank the many people who have made me
sensitive to language, caused me to care about writing and
teaching, kept me curious, and
helped make time and space for me to write this book.

CONTENTS

INTRODUCTION

THE ENGLISH DEPARTMENT OFFICES WERE ON THE THIRD FLOOR OF the library, on the end near fraternity row. I climbed slowly up the stairs, planting each foot deliberately on the worn marble treads. At the top, to the left, was the secretary's desk. It was a few minutes before five. I stood quietly in front of her, happy to let seconds pass as I waited for her to notice me. When she finally looked up, I asked her where Dr. B's office was. She gave me the number, glanced at the clock, and began to put the plastic cover on her typewriter. "I don't know if he's still there," she said, shrugging on her coat. I gave her a little smile. I hoped he wasn't—in fact, I was counting on it.

The hallway was dim, still, lined by wooden doors darkened with old varnish. Closed now, they were littered with evidence of the academic world: notes, cartoons, and envelopes with students' papers jutting out were taped or thumb-tacked all over them. I walked slowly, quietly, not wanting to break the stillness. My heart rose into my throat—Dr. B's door was ajar, and he was at his desk. He looked up, his eyebrows raising in surprise, then he stood, opening the door wide for me.

"You said to come and see you," I whispered.

"Yes, yes," he said, "come in."

I was a sophomore, a first-generation college student, struggling in my English major, struggling with the language, the ways of writing, learning, and living at college. Dr. B. was notoriously tough and equally well-liked. I had notebooks full of his words—scribbled verbatim—and I also had a stack of papers with ever-decreasing grades. On the last one, he had written: "F+ —come and see me."

So there I was, though I hadn't planned on actually seeing him. I had thought I might just miss him, but would leave a note saying,

"Sorry I missed you. I'll try to catch you some other time." The secretary would have been able to vouch that I had really been there, doing what his end note had demanded. But it was all messed up now. Though I could hide in his class—keep my head down, take notes furiously, laugh when others did, look at my book—now it was just the two of us in a small office.

The sounds of the fraternity boys shouting obscenities and insults and laughing loudly rose up through the window as Dr. B. pulled a chair over near his desk. I handed him my paper silently and sat down. He held the paper out for us both to read while I held my chin in my hands and let my long hair fall forward to shield my face. He began with the first page, and line by line, word by word, he showed me where I'd failed, used the wrong construction, argued the reverse of my point, or made no sense at all. From time to time he nodded his head violently, and his little reading glasses fell from his nose to his chest, clicking as they struck a button on his shirt. I could see this through the veil of my hair, but I wouldn't look openly at him, wouldn't let him see me.. I couldn't breathe. My chest and throat were full, and I stared unblinkingly at the monstrously wrong type-written pages I'd worked hard on to make neat and inconspicuous—just as I'd worked hard to make myself inconspicuous in his class.

Finally he was silent. I remained still. I knew he wanted me to respond, to talk to him, but I had no words. After a little bit, he sat up straight, sighed deeply, leaned forward again, and said something like: "Look. There are some good ideas here. But they're not phrased right. See? This paragraph right here for example. This is interesting. But listen to how it could sound." He began to read, changing it subtly or radically as he read. As I followed along, I saw that the words weren't all mine, but they sounded right somehow, they sounded like what I read in books and articles and the papers written by my wealthy and better-spoken classmates, sounded like what professors sounded like. My ideas, his words.

Suddenly I was standing, and Dr. B. was looking up in surprise. The conference wasn't over, but I was thanking him, stuffing my paper into my backpack, telling him how helpful he'd been as I turned and whirled back through the doorway, half walking, half running down the dim hall. I was afraid he'd follow me and ask what was wrong, but I was crying and didn't want him to know. Besides, I didn't know exactly what was wrong. I banged the ladies room door open, dropped my pack in a stall, and leaned against the door. I didn't know if I was crying because I was so stupid that I'd made a nice man—my teacher—frustrated to the point of sighing and giving me an F+, or whether I was relieved that for the first time, my ideas had been matched to the words that carried weight, and maybe I could start again from this one hybrid paragraph and rebuild myself. In the dark stall, I wept in stupidity and relief.

* * * * *

The poems I'd turned in for the week, now scrawled all over and stained with coffee, lay on my professor's lap. I remember two of them. One was about a bank robbery gone bad, each section of the poem moving further into the mind of one of the robbers. They were all male characters, and their words and thoughts were full of obscenities and sexual slurs. In the other poem, I used the metaphor of a suicidal "jumper" to explore a first sexual experience—mine, as I spoke to a younger sister. The teacher handed me the poems and asked me to read them aloud. He leaned back, eyes shut, listening. When I was done, he rolled his chair over to me, close enough that our legs touched. He looked at me in surprise, laughing a little, and asked me where I'd learned to use obscenity like that. I, too, was astonished, realizing for the first time that my disguise—a privileged coed from a "good" family—was successful, that he couldn't see the "real" me. After the astonishment, I was afraid. I could feel my face burning as I wondered what I should say. That I learned to swear from my mother? That in the summer, when I worked on an island with lobstermen, we talked easily, our speech peppered with obscenity? Finally, I managed to joke, "Jeeze, I wasn't born a nun, you know!" As he laughed and said, "I know, but-" I cut him off, asking an acceptable question in an eager tone: "But does it work?"

We talked in the yellow light of the little office along the same dark hallway I'd fled down a year before. I don't know if he was as aware as I of how close he was sitting to me, of how hard I struggled to find ways to answer his request for "more detail" in my poem, ways that would keep us firmly teacher and student, not friends, not equals, not anything other than what we'd constructed in class. I don't know if *he* struggled as he tried to describe how a man might think in the situations I presented to him. I know I cursed myself silently for giving him these poems, even as I knew that I had no choice. He was my teacher, I had to give him poems, I was going to be graded by him on my writing, and these were my best. I can't recall exact words now, but the scene remains, almost tactile—our words brushing against each other, the warmth where our legs touched, the coffee-stained pages rough in my hands, the onion skin paper flickering as we breathed.

* * * * *

I begin with these two memories because they hold great power for me. They have stayed with me for almost two decades, these two relatively brief speech events in a genre of talk which supposedly reduces the tensions of the classroom, lets teachers and students get to know each other, and pushes against those traditional student-teacher power relationships. They embody some of the hidden tensions of conferencing for both students and teachers, and they illustrate some of the problems and frustrations that teachers, myself included, have long voiced about conferencing. Silent students. Writing that is unaffected by conferencing. Resistant students. Open assumptions and hidden fears. For crying out loud, teachers lament, what was going through her head while I was telling her how to fix this paper?! I can't say whether these two examples represent "good" or "bad" conferences; certainly, the first was a turning point in my academic career, and the second a moment when cultural constructions of class, status, and gender stirred the surface of the talk like the backs of hungry fish. They are moments I've returned to when I've asked students to write about their best or worst conferences and I write with them, still not sure into which category to place these conferences.

When I've looked out my door to see three students waiting to conference and my schedule shows twelve after that; when my most difficult student—the one closest to failing, the one who tries and tries and is always on the wrong page, has no draft, can't find the paper—appears late and moments before another student is scheduled, I am reminded of the fear and tensions of my own conferences as a student. Now I'm the one with the chair that rolls and lets me control the geography of the office; I have to ask for more detail; I have to understand resistance, desire, and fear from a perspective I could only guess at—which I didn't—as a student. The problem is, I don't always do these things very well. Like most teachers, I am not merely self-trained at conferencing, but trained by those (in this case, all white men over my four years as an undergraduate and mostly men, all white, as a graduate student) who held my papers in their hands and talked earnestly to me in words they thought or hoped I would understand. I bring those experiences—most blurred and internalized, a few stark and sharp as the two I've recounted here—with me to my writing conferences. They are now framed in a feminist perspective I didn't have at eighteen or twenty-two or even later. What seemed perfectly natural, woven tapestry-like into the fabric of the first conference, was the fraternity jousting that formed a backdrop for the control Dr. B. had of my paper, my physical space, my words. It also seemed natural at the time of the second conference that I would be writing persona poems in which I adopted the voice of a man, and that the professor would tell me how men thought even in a poem about my own sexual experience.

These are aspects of conferencing that I can interrogate, things I am now sensitive to and conscious of. But the lessons I have learned from my teaching models, from the culture in which I grew up (white, female, working poor, suburban/rural, North American) are less easily noticed. I can reflect on them here while I write: in the real time of conferencing, they are more elusive but no less powerful. If we look back on the two scenes I began with, there is much that is missing; they are sketched and shaded broadly. What were the words Dr. B. used as he dissected my paper? How, finally, did I phrase answers to the questions about my poems, questions which I remember being carefully worded but pressuring? One of the powers of narrative is its movement to which we submit, and thus its ability to escape scrutiny, to avoid being held still and examined. The narratives I've written of my own student conferences are powerful because they are part of a chain, constructed in some ways to evoke similar responses and evoked by stories from my own students and the students of other instructors. They are emotionally "whole" for me, but for analytical purposes, they are incomplete. The narratives we tell each other as teachers who are struggling with our conferences also move along to what appears to be an inevitable conclusion: frustration and often failure. When we turn with delight to a colleague and talk about a wonderful conference, it is often with amazement. But successful or unsuccessful, these are usually stories told on the fly, in a hallway or over a quick cup of coffee, and they remain unreflected upon. Conferencing is something we do, but unexamined, it remains something we do not understand and thus cannot improve.

Writing a book like this is not simply one of those "school things," as my father would say. Instead it is driven by my desire to understand and come to grips with the fear and frustration of my conferences as a student and my continuing frustration with conferencing as a teacher. I sat silently in my classes and conferences, aware that if I opened my mouth I would reveal something "wrong" about myself. I listened intently for clues to the language I needed in order to respond "intelligently;" I tentatively used language picked up in the classroom on a hit-or-miss basis in my papers and waited for the written comments to teach me things I had no language to even ask about. My class and gender, so different from those who simultaneously "conversed" with me and evaluated me on my ability to "converse" with them, became a part of me I needed to deny or exercise control over. I remember clearly making the decision to say to a professor, "Really?" instead of the more "colorful" and, to me, natural "Get outta heayah!"

In the chapters that follow, I will address many of the problems that teachers and students experience in conferencing. In many ways, it is artificial to separate out one problem from another, for conferences, like the people who construct them, are complex. Any problems or frustrations or confusions we experience in conferencing have multiple sources and solutions. But in order to look for solutions, I've needed to isolate and clarify problems. In chapter one, I examine one of the fundamental problems with conferencing—the conflicting paradigms which fill our literature and from which we may draw our visions of conferencing. Are conferences conversations? Are they teaching? If we can see conferencing as something separate from teaching, as a genre of speech itself, we may be able to raise new and productive questions. How do we define this speech genre, and what are the implications of that definition for our practice? What are our purposes in conferencing? And how do our beliefs about the roles of students and teachers affect the ways in which we shape conferences? I consider how changing the focus from the written texts we usually talk about to the spoken text that is the conference can lead us to new ways of thinking about this important part of our practice. In chapter two, I examine the ways in which the asymmetry of conferencing—the differing power status of teacher and student—can lead to frustrating situations. While the first chapter deals with this asymmetry in theory, the second chapter deals with it in practice. What happens when we don't realize our own power?

When does direction become directive? When do we choose to use our power and why? In chapter three, I look at how gender complicates conferencing. Of course, what we are coming to know more clearly is how "gendered" language is also language that reflects power relations. Simply because we have supposedly replaced the confines of the classroom with the linguistically less constrained parameters of the conference, gender does not disappear for either teacher or student, and our conference talk is marked by the social and linguistic evidence of gender roles in many ways. Chapter four explores the difficulties of cross cultural communication. How does racial difference between parties—with all the social differences that usually entails in this country—affect conferencing? How do we or need we shift conferencing practice for students from other countries or home cultures? As classrooms become more diverse in both culture and ability, teachers are turning to conferences to help individual students. What issues do they need to consider as the relationship becomes one-to-one? In chapter five, I look at the affective dimension of conferencing. It is easy to forget sometimes that we chose our field because of how we felt about our own teachers, how we were moved or inspired by what we read or heard, how we were attracted to a certain approach to understanding the world around us. We get caught up in what students should or need to "know" and forget that knowing and feeling aren't so easily separated. Participants in conferences come in with feelings, but those feelings aren't usually acknowledged as valid topics for discussion. Finally, in chapter six, I explore a vision of conferencing that is informed by critical reflection, critical pedagogy, and what I know about language at this point in my life. To construct this chapter, I returned mentally to the faculty lounge where new teachers and experienced teachers sit and talk, where new approaches and possible solutions can rise from the ashes of "crash and burn" conferences through an alchemy of lore, practice, research, and hope.

Throughout this book, I work within a framework informed by tenets of critical pedagogy and sociolinguistics, particularly critical discourse analysis. I draw heavily on my own experience and research on the language of conferencing, assuming, as most critical discourse analysts do, that the structures of society—our relationships to one another—are revealed in our language interactions or, just as importantly, our lack of interaction. Both critical pedagogy and critical discourse analysis are interested in laying bare power structures that limit or suppress access to knowledge, to public speech, to various social, political, and personal domains; that support the institution-alization of "prestige" and the value system that accompanies it; that help isolate large groups of people who are unable for a number of reasons to participate fully as informed citizens. This theoretical position is always, however, linked to my own experiences as a female, as a child growing up among the working poor, as a student who struggled to fit in socially and academically, as a graduate stu-dent who searched for years before realizing what she loved to do, as a teacher of writing and literature and language, and as a writer who writes from institutional compulsion, disciplinary excitement and dialogue, and personal need. Our past is always with us, and these positions and experiences are simultaneously devalued and powerful. I don't hesitate to draw on them in this book, and I don't hesitate to ask questions I can't answer and perhaps can't even properly articu-late or frame. For me, this is the beginning of a dialogue on an important issue. I have in the past been afraid to ask some of my questions about conferencing and teaching, as I know my colleagues have been. If it's true that much of what goes on in our classrooms is hidden except for the occasional required observation by a peer or administrator and what we choose to share with colleagues, then practically *all* of what goes on in conferences is also hidden, private. Most of what we have learned or "know" about conferencing has gone unquestioned, unexamined, for it is presented as such a simple part of teaching practice that the least able of us should be able to do well. In order to accept that commonly held belief, we must deny our own experiences or fit them, willy-nilly, into the paradigms we've been given. If we do so, however, we will never learn.

In many places throughout the book, I refer to and draw on research I've conducted on my own conferencing and the confer-ences of my colleagues. As I explain in more detail in chapter one, I became interested in conferencing after analyzing six of my own con-ferences: three with female, all white and traditional-aged first-year students, and three with males, again all traditional-aged first-year students, one of whom was African-American. This initial research led me to a larger study of fourteen conferences between first-year students and their teachers, ranging from graduate assistants to a full professor. Four male teachers and three female teachers conference with six male and eight female students (see Appendix A). All but one participant was white. Not all students responded to my request for demographic data, but of those who did, all indicated they were middle- to upper-class with the exception of a white female, who indicated that she was working class: her father, she said, "worked hard with his hands" to support them. The conferences were audio-taped and transcribed, coded for particular features and a frequency count of features by teacher/student role and gender was done. Certainly, it was a small study of a homogeneous group. But like most teacher research, it grew from an immediate context—I discovered a problem I wanted to explore and possibly resolve. The students represent the demographics where I was teaching, and they and their teachers were willing to help. I use this research as a jumping-off point to raise questions about conferencing, and illustrate with excerpts from the transcripts some of the difficulties teachers and students face in constructing successful, meaningful conferences.

The title of the book reflects the tensions of writing conferences and my concern with the structure that undergirds them. We desire for so much to happen in conferences with our students, maybe more than we will admit to ourselves. And we often find ourselves caught, unable to balance teaching and talking, either unable to leave the platform and step out on the tightwire or rushing because our lives depend upon it to the safety of the opposite end of the wire. I thought at length about incorporating into the title of this book a reference to one student's—Dana's—off-hand, vaguely negative summary of Hemingway's "Big Two-Hearted River" as a "story of a man who went on a fishing trip." This was partly because I am drawn to images that resonate for me, and this one became a controlling image as I wrote. I think, as a teacher, I've always felt that conferencing with my students about their writing helped bring me closer to them somehow. But as I listened to the tape of Dana and Eric's conference, I laughed along with Eric as he rephrased Dana's comment to "a long story about fishing." It was a moment when I realized how great a distance I had come from being a student myself, how imbedded in professorial power and knowledge I was. I felt ashamed that I could laugh at the "ignorance" of a student, embarassed that I accepted the professor's rephrasing, which poked fun at the student for the very problem she had come to speak with him about: how to "be insightful." Yet listening to myself laugh, feeling this awkward moment, I realized I could create a new role, a new place for me to stand as I thought through all these conferences. After all, wasn't I after the same thing as Dana—to be insightful about my own teaching, my own conferencing? I suspect that the readers of this book are themselves all fishing in the waters of teaching and learning, of language and power and change, and that we are open and excited by the possibilities, by playing an active role in an on-going story where what we really catch and what we create are open to discussion. And where the analogy breaks down, there is more complexity and even excitement, for students are our partners in this practice. We can fish alone, but we cannot confer alone.

If the composition community has embraced a pedagogical technique that it has not fully explored, it has done so on the basis of the most humane assumptions: it allows teachers and students to enter each other's worlds, it affords teachers the opportunity to provide individualized help to students, and it extends collaboration beyond the classroom, beyond the peer-writing group. And yet, every time I have asked students to write about either their best or worst conferencing experiences, the great majority of them choose to write about their worst. Some admit that they can't think of a best, only a "least worst." Writing along with the students, I, too, find that I have many "worst" conferences to write about, but have only a scanty cupboard of "bests" as both teacher and student. What occurs between the best of intentions that we began with and the often ineffective or even negative outcomes that students and teachers report? I hope, in the rest of this book, to come a little closer to answering that question and to offer some suggestions to create more "bests" for all participants in conferences.

CHAPTER ONE

Conversation, Teaching, and Points in Between

The Confusion of Conferencing

I BEGAN STUDYING MY OWN CONFERENCING PRACTICE MANY YEARS ago, while I was still a graduate student. I'll admit that I chose that particular project for my research course because I was smug in my belief that any examination would show the professor and my classmates how fair, honest, critical, thoughtful, reflective, and even nurturing I was. It would show that I could connect with each student individually and personally. But what I learned from analyzing transcripts of my conferences is how great a distance lay between my image and my words, my goals and my practice. Despite any perceptions I may have had about the "personal" nature of student-teacher conferences, the academic patterning of the classroom and the cultural patterning which the classroom reinscribes carried over to my conferences and undermined my efforts at equalizing power and engaging in real conversation and cooperative learning.

I looked at only six of my conferences, but my first response was horror. For example, two female students who came in with ideas for papers and detailed plans repeatedly dismissed their knowledge and work with "I don't know." One said she was "running off at the mouth." I rather feebly said, "Oh, no, these are good," but I didn't spend any significant time exploring or addressing their negative self-generalizations; I had other things I wanted to get to. Female students didn't use much of the disciplinary terminology I'd worked so hard to make a part of the classroom talk; substitutes for a simple word like "paragraph" were "right here" or "parts" of the paper, and "support" was "put more stuff in." I found that, in return, I didn't use any of that language with them. When they asked for help, asked for clear and specific direction, I didn't give it to them. I made them jump through the same hoops I'd had to jump through. One young woman admitted that she didn't "know how to say things," an admission that covered both the paper we were discussing and our discussion itself. I let it hang in the air, and in frustration, ultimately agreed with her. Male students didn't have to ask for help—I offered it. One threw about disciplinary-specific words like rice at a wedding and I responded enthusiastically to him. Later examination of the transcript seemed to reveal that he didn't have much idea what the words meant. Another confident student I praised as a "Writer" with a capital "W," even though his ideas and writing weren't significantly better than one of the more hesitant women. Yet a black student seemed to anticipate challenges to his ideas, immediately justifying them even as I opened my mouth.

If my first response was to be shocked, my second was to attempt to mitigate my shame and embarrassment by thinking, "Surely others conference as badly as I do!" This led me in two directions. One was to ask, "What's going on with conferencing?" and begin gathering tapes of conferences from willing colleagues and students, analyzing them critically to begin describing conferencing. The other direction was to go back, to try and determine what had led me to my own practice. I went back to the images of conferencing that fill the pages of books and articles in composition and which helped me to construct a picture of my conference practice that, unfortunately, existed only in my head. I realized that many of these descriptions of conferences were visionary, that they drew pictures with such broad strokes that I had retained the outline of the image but provided a substance drawn from my own previous conferencing experiences, my own locations.

The widespread disciplinary assumptions about conferencing appear to be that conferences are either conversations about writing—casual, comfortable, rapport-building sessions—or a form of individualized teaching, sensitive to the needs of the student in the chair across from the instructor. What I want to show is that these assumptions and the images of conferencing that emerge from them are at best naive, and at worst, potentially harmful. One way to do this is to become conscious of and understand the linguistic structures of conversation, teaching, and learning and the ways in which these structures are part of larger cultural and social structures. Conferencing is an asymmetrical language interaction, drawing its rules from both the discourse of the classroom and from casual conversation. But teaching and conversation are (and create) very different and often problematic contexts and relationships. In a profession dedicated to both preserving tradition and effecting change, it's not surprising to find such a contradiction. But, simply put, the structure of conversation and the structure of traditional teaching talk are quite different: the purpose of communication is different, the speakers' roles are different, and the status of speakers is different. We cannot simply move from one to the other. It is not a mere physical act like shifting from one foot to another. If one participant thinks a conference is a conversation and the other thinks it is teaching, then there is going to be confusion: who speaks when? What topics are appropriate? What role should each play? I'd like in this chapter to examine the contradictory nature of those speech structures and thus our images of conferencing, and to offer some suggestions to teachers for using what they learn about conversation, teaching, and genres of speech. To do so, I'm going to consider how conferencing is conceived of in typical composition and pedagogy sources and how theories of social constructionism and sociolinguistic approaches to conferencing might help us reconsider and understand some of our difficulties with this practice.

Generations of Conferences

Our understanding and conception of writing conferences is poised on the brink of change after a long period in which it has remained, beneath the surface anyway, fundamentally untouched by the changes in writing instruction. Why do writing teachers conference with students? We conference because it is efficient: we can say more about a paper than we can write in the same amount of time, and we can deal individually with the problems of a student and thus not impede the progress of an entire class or even a writing group. We conference because we believe it is effective: students learn more from oral responses than written ones; if a conference is timed appropriately, the teacher can intervene in the writing process at the points where help is most needed; it gives students an interested listener and a chance to discuss their writing with the real audience for it; and it provides motivation. We conference because we believe it will help our students discover "things" about themselves and the world around them, because we have something to say about that world of which we are a part and we can't say all of our piece in a classroom.

Conferences also make more visible processes that are usually hidden from teachers or students. We ask students what they were thinking about when they wrote this line, when they suddenly switched to a new topic or changed their writing voice. Conferences help demystify the process of evaluation for students as the teacher reads through and responds in a variety of ways to the draft while the student listens and watches. Finally, we conference because it helps us get to know our students better. In conferences, students can express both academic and personal concerns, can tell us the stories of their lives as they discuss what prompted and informed their writing. As teachers, we can respond to those personal elements confidentially and with feeling that we may not care (or dare) to show in the classroom

Such claims for the success and value in conferencing are broad and long-standing. More than two decades ago, Squire and Applebee (1968, cited in Duke, 44) asserted that: "Perhaps the most successful practice in the teaching of composition has been the regular conference to discuss problems and progress of the individual student" (254). More recently, Witte, Meyer, Miller, and Faigley (1982, cited in Freedman and Katz, 60), state their finding that directors of first-year writing programs nationwide believe conferences are "the most successful part of their teaching programs."

But these claims for success need to be examined more closely. Certainly, our own experiences tell us that conferences are not always so successful—but what are the criteria for success? If we follow accounts of conferencing over the last three decades, what we see are largely narratives, exhortations, and guidelines presented uncritically. Lad Tobin (1990) helps us consider the slowly-developing conference structure, making a distinction between what he calls "first generation" and "second generation" conferences, and looking ahead to a third (or perhaps a "next"?!) generation informed by recent theories and debate about the social construction of knowledge and the acquisition of language. First generation conferences, he argues, follow the lead of Roger Garrison and other early supporters of "one-to-one" teaching—brief conferences held regularly with students as they work on papers individually. These conferences are highly directive, with teachers setting the agenda and dispensing information to students who receive it passively, rewrite their work, and return for another brief conference. Descriptions of conferencing during this early period make clear how powerfully the teacher controls the event. Garrison writes that "It is better for a student to be an apprentice at your side for five minutes than a disciple at your feet for five months" (69). Knapp (1976) echoes Garrison's imagery, referring to the student as an "acolyte" and the teacher as a "priest" (47). Hiatt (1975) problematizes easy claims for success and learning in one-to-one tutorials, but still posits a conferencing relationship with students that is clearly teacher-centered, with all agency given to the instructor. "Willing scholars" receive passively the few comments on grammar and mechanics that they need; the "unwilling scholar" must be "captured" and tamed. Without attention to differences in knowledge and terminology, such a student is "held at bay" (39).

Second generation conferences are—theoretically—non-directive; Tobin sees Donald Murray as the exemplar of this approach. Tied to the growing use of a process approach to writing, second generation conferences are student-centered and focus on active learning as opposed to passive absorption. In such conferences, the goal is to let the student set the agenda and do the talking, while the teacher asks the right questions to help students discover their topics and evaluate their own writing. Like first generation conferences, these are problem-solving meetings; however, the problems are identified and solved by students, with the expert guidance of the teacher. But, Tobin argues, the process approach to conference teaching rather quickly became "ritualized." The text of conferences became as idealized as the written student text instructors had in mind in first-generation conferences. And, in fact, Murray himself (1985) states that "Students need to know *the* dynamics of *the* conference: the student is expected to say something about the draft; the teacher is expected to listen, read the draft, and respond to what the student said; the student is expected to listen to the teacher and respond" (152, emphases mine).

Duke (1975) for example, draws on theories and practices of Rogerian reflection and questioning in his discussion of conferencing. He argues that if the conference is "truly student-centered and non-directive," Rogerian questions will help a student see where she should go next in a writing a paper.

> This kind of structuring, or focusing . . . provides a sense of security for the student; he no longer has to worry about the direction of the conference and he is given a specific task on which to focus . . . also avoided here is the unplanned, rambling monologue which all too often characterizes the meeting between student and teacher and only results in confusing the student further. (45)

Somehow, the non-directive teacher has retained all the agency in this conference; he structures it, provides security for the student, relieves him of worry, gives him a task to focus on, and ensures that he is not confused by either his own talk or the teacher's.

Dissatisfied with both these paradigms, Tobin looks forward to an evolution that acknowledges the complexity of conferencing, that sees "dynamics" less as a boilerplate for interaction and more as a social relationship. He calls for "an approach that takes into account the dynamic aspects of each writing conference: the student's relationship to the text, the teacher's relationship to the text, and the student and teacher's relationship to each other" (99). Tobin's tentative description of a third generation conference shares common elements with the relationship Donald Murray calls a "trialogue," where the text is the focus point of the conference, and the student and teacher speak of the text and check responses *with* the text (Murray, 1985, 150). But Tobin's vision goes beyond that, certainly, in its concern for the student-teacher relationship, the tension that results from the differences in power and expectations of participants, and in its call for the "careful studying of our students and ourselves" (100).

If a third generation of conferencing has appeared, it is keeping a low profile. What *has* appeared over the past decade are examinations of conferencing that begin to apply theories of feminism, collaborative learning, and social constructionism, and which apply sociolinguistic methodologies and findings to critique the anecdotal portrayals of conferencing that have provided the foundation for further practice.

Tobin's diachronous distinctions between generations of conferences are clearly tied to changes in composition pedagogy, from traditional approaches emphasizing the unproblematic transmission of knowledge to process approaches emphasizing the social nature of knowledge to even more recent approaches asserting the social construction of knowledge and denying the "nature" of anything. But the differences he sees between the first two generations seem superficial. While the metaphors of priest and acolyte, civilizer and barbarian change to those of counselor and client, master and apprentice, the power relations these metaphors speak to remain unchanged and largely unexamined, and issues of gender, race, and class remain invisible. The evolutionary spin which Tobin puts on his history of conferencing touches positive chords in readers: we *are* getting better, we think to ourselves in relief, we *are* sensitive to changes around us and adapt to them as needed to be good teachers and citizens. In its new clothing, however, the conference DNA still twists in a familiar double helix, genetically unchanged.

Cognitivism and Social Constructionism

One reason, perhaps, for the lack of critical examination of conferences is that until recently, many teachers have brought with them to conferencing the assumptions of a traditional cognitive theory of knowledge. This could be so for a number of reasons. While recent, more critical research on conferences and pedagogy draws on theories of social construction and social reproduction, many students of secondary education and most English department teaching assistants receive little to no training specifically focused on conferencing. The social constructionist theories they read about and may experience in some classrooms are not applied to other situations connected to teaching. Thus cognitive theories remain the "default" for many teachers as they consider their conferencing practice.

Ken Bruffee (1986) offers some helpful distinctions between cognitive approaches to knowledge and learning and a social constructionist approach. When we speak in cognitive terms about knowledge, we make several assumptions. One, of course, is that with the "mirror and inner eye" which are part of the human brain, we can "see" what is "out there" and then contemplate it: "The mirror reflects outer reality. The inner eye contemplates that reflection." Another assumption is that processes that occur within the mind are objectifiable, measurable. A third assumption is that "the individual self is the matrix of all thought." Finally, a fourth assumption is that knowledge is problematic and incomplete, for there is a gap between the mirror and the inner eye. Bruffee reminds us that "cognitive work is based on the assumption that writing is primarily an individual act. A writer's language originates within the inner reaches of the individual mind. We use language primarily to express ideas generated in the mind and to communicate them to other individual human minds in the 'social context'" (776-77, 784).

When these assumptions are applied to composition and particularly to conferencing, we can see how they affect the ways we perceive the function and structure of a conference. Jacobs and Karliner (1977) write that one function of the conference is to help the student "discover and develop ideas" (489), while Rose (1982) states that "in a live encounter, students can sometimes be prodded to discover more about what they really have to say." For Rose, the conference also "provides an opportunity to actually see minds at work" (326). Freedman and Sperling (1985) argue that "the student presumably is to come away from a conference having been given at least something from the teacher" (111-12). These statements indicate just how strongly the cognitivist tradition shapes our interaction in conferencing. The reification of knowledge—its conceptualization as an object that can be given—runs through such accounts of conferencing. Metaphors which would help readers reconceive the conference along lines that are more concerned with the construction of knowledge than the transmission of knowledge are rare.

This is a hard mindset to shake. Like so many of us teaching now, I am the product of the practice such theory helps create. Urgings from professors to "think deeper" and maybe "discover" what I really thought about subject "X" always made me close my eyes to the world around me and try to look inward to learn. But in fact, as I recall conferences with professors, I realize that I did the eye-closing thing after much discussion, and when I responded with my "discovery" it was almost always to say, "Thanks, I never thought about all that in those terms before." My knowledge of "X" had not been discovered deep within, but had been constructed by reconsidering personal beliefs in a new context provided by my meaningful contact with a teacher. That "thing" that was my knowledge was constantly being socially constructed.

Bruffee juxtaposes cognitivist assumptions and social constructionism in order to underscore their differences. Social constructionism challenges the assumption of foundational truths and argues instead that knowledge, ideas, theories, and "facts" are constructs of language which represent the consensus of beliefs held by particular communities. It denies "ownership" of knowledge or ideas; rather, it "understands knowledge and the authority of knowledge as community-generated, community-maintaining symbolic artifacts" (777). The problematic nature of knowledge as understood by traditional cognitivists is no longer an issue if language and knowledge are seen as one and the same. Finally, and most importantly for my movement in this discussion of conflicting paradigms of conferencing, Bruffee asserts that when we talk about the process of thinking, of seeing the mind at work, "such terms do not refer to anything universal, objectifiable, or measurable. Rather, they are a way of talking about talking. Social constructionism assumes, that is, that thinking is an internalized version of conversation. Anything we say about the way thinking works is conversation about another conversation: talk about talk" (777).

Here, Bruffee is drawing on Lev Vygotsky's concept of thought as "inner speech," as internalized conversation. Vygotsky's theory is one of language acquisition; social constructionists see this as synonymous with knowledge acquisition. Our inner speech is the result of many conversations; when we re-externalize that speech (in writing, for Bruffee), we construct it to take part in a particular community, to "know" what they know. Social constructionist work in composition is "based on the assumption that writing is primarily a social act. A writer's language originates with the community to which he or she belongs. We use language primarily to join communities we do not yet belong to and to cement our membership in communities we already belong to" (784). In accounts of conferencing that focus on the student's written text and the consequences of conference talk on that text—that is, the majority of literature on conferencing—the dynamics of the speech event are subordinated to the goal of the event. But in a sociolinguistic approach, the talk becomes the text. Bruffee reminds us that "collaborative learning is related to social construction in that it assumes learning occurs among persons rather than between a person and things" (787).

Speech ethnographers, sociolinguists, and social constructionists support in varying degrees the belief that the "self" is as much a linguistic and communal construct as any other concept. As I type these words, I am reminded again of my conference with Dr. B., of my conferences with other professors in which I wanted to use the language that would mark me as a member of the academy, or at least of being worthy to enter that community. Simultaneously, I was ashamed of and yet clung to the language that identified me as "poor" and "provincial." Even now, as I speak with family, I speak in ways that remind us of my ties to them and my role as part of their community. I am reluctant to use the language I use with my colleagues. This is not simply because it is so similar to the language my family has always associated with groups of people who have oppressed and insulted them (lawyers, bankers, bureaucrats of all kinds), but because it is confusing to me and confuses "me," highlighting the multiple selves that I usually conceive of as a unified self. I belong to communities that do not usually overlap, and must find some language to bridge the gaps between what is "true" and valued in each community.

When I was younger (and still today), one of my heroes was Jacques Cousteau. And as I tried to enliven the after-dinner chores of my two older sisters and myself, I would reach down into the sink full of dishes, swirl my hand around, and narrate, in my best bad French accent, "Phillippe dives quickly. In ze depps of ze merky watta, he discovehrs lost tweashehre. Carefully, he bwings up an ainsient, encwusted fook, ze wehmains of a final, watery deenah." Although I was the youngest, I suddenly had all the status. No one could "do" Jacques Cousteau like I could. I was the focus of attention. No insults, no teasing, none of the sibling snubbing that I often endured. What I could do with words changed the way we interacted; I had, momentarily, reconstructed our relationship. (Who knows how this paragraph has reconstructed my relationship with readers!) Sociolinguistics takes as its focus the talk between parties: how that talk is constructed, why it is constructed in certain ways, and how that talk reconstructs the relationship between speakers, and speakers and their communities. It takes only a small jump for me to move from social constructionism to sociolinguistics—and critical sociolinguistics at that. I was eager to find conferencing studies that considered talk-as-text and context. But what I have discovered is that most studies of conferencing still do not apply what we've learned from sociolinguistics, despite the obvious: conferences are identified more by the talk that occurs than the written texts under discussion.

Conferencing, Conversation, and Teaching

As a discipline, we are clear that conferencing is not just a part of teaching, it *is* teaching. It is "individualized instruction" (Carnicelli, 1985), a way of "teaching" students to react to their work (Murray, 1979), and a "popular and seemingly effective pedagogical event" (Freedman and Sperling, 1985). Regardless of what we may know about our students or they about us, no matter how many times we have met them outside the classroom, in the conference they are usually learners and we are teachers. These roles may shift slightly: Murray writes that his students teach him, that he is a learner in many cases, but he writes this with some astonishment, with the tone of someone who is happily and continually amazed to see the traditional relationship between teacher and student reversed. However, what is also clear in his narratives about conferencing is that students do not see *themselves* as teachers, only learners.

So conferencing is teaching. But its language is perceived as neither a lecture nor a discussion (in a teaching context, "discussion" seems to mean to both teachers and students the inclusion of more than two voices (Black, 1992)). Instead, we read that

> a writing conference is a conversation between a student and a teacher about a student's paper. Since it is, or should be, a genuine conversation, it follows no set pattern; it simply evolves as the two parties talk" (Carnicelli, 1985).
>
> Everyday conversation forms the substructure for interactive composition instruction; everyday conversational misfires form the context for confusions in student revisions. (Feehan, 1989)
>
> These conferences should have the tone of conversations. They are not mini-lectures but the working talk of fellow writers sharing their experience with the writing process. (Murray, 1985)

The paradigm of the "conference-as-conversation" permeates accounts of conferencing. As you can imagine, however, it does not do so without some tension. After all, consider immediately the differences between talk among teachers in the faculty lounge and talk between teachers and students in conferences. Warning bells should go off as we read about conference "conversation." But our desire to meet on more equal ground with our students muffles the sound. For example, Murray goes on to say: "At times, of course, they will be teacher and student, master and apprentice, if you want, but most of the time they will be remarkably close to peers, because each writer, no matter how experienced, begins again with each draft" (1985).

Murray's perception of the teacher having the power to control the nature of the conference is in opposition to his democratic impulse to flatten out status differences between students and teachers under the weight of the role of "writer." Along with the assumption of teacher control ("if you want") is the assumption that there are reasons why a teacher would shift from conversation to teaching. Yet there is no discussion of the benefits of one form of talk over the others for teachers, students, or both. Thomas Newkirk (1989) simultaneously warns teachers to set an agenda, "or a conference can run on aimlessly...So much student talk could be digressive" and writes: "Most conferences seem casual, supportive...But the seemingly effortless, conversational quality of conferences belies their complexity, for both teacher and student are filling paradoxical roles" (317, 326). And Kenneth Bruffee makes the point that "productive conversation for all of us is most likely to occur with people we regard as equals, members of our own community. Conversation with members of another community is always somewhat strained, something of a performance" (1985, 4).

Our confusion between conversation and teaching has led to a variety of conflicting claims, warnings, guidelines, and questions that need to be answered. Conversations do not have "agendas" that we must be wary of straying from. How can student talk be "digressive" if there is no agenda? Why isn't teacher talk digressive? Are students our equals? Are we members of the same community in important ways? When I compare the kind of talk going on between my students (especially my younger students) as I enter my classroom to the kind of talk I have had in conferences with those same students, I find it difficult to say that I have had a conversation with my student in conference; I am sure that the two situations produced different kinds of talk.

Most research on conversation is based on the work of Sacks, Schlegoff, and Jefferson (1974). Working from extensive transcripts of naturally occurring conversation, they attempted to characterize its simplest form. For Sacks, et al., the turn-taking mechanism of conversation is both context-free (it always occurs, regardless of the context) and context-sensitive; that is, the length of turns and their order will differ between kinds of speech exchanges—debates, argument, ceremony—and will be shaped by social organization, as an "economy" in which parties may hold different speech capital and thus be permitted to speak at varying lengths. They list the following characteristics as fundamental to conversation:

1. Speaker change recurs, or at least occurs.
2. Overwhelmingly, one party talks at a time.
3. Occurrences of more than one speaker at a time are common, but brief.
4. Transitions (from one turn to the next) with no gap and no overlap are common. Together with transition characterized by a slight gap or slight overlap, they make up the vast majority of transitions.
5. Turn order is not fixed, but varies.
6. Turn size is not fixed, but varies.
7. Length of conversation is not specified in advance.

8. What parties say is not specified in advance.
9. Relative distribution of turns is not specified in advance.
10. Number of parties can vary.
11. Talk can be continuous or discontinuous.
12. Turn-allocation techniques are obviously used. A current speaker may select a next speaker (as when he addresses a question to another party); or parties may self-select in starting to talk.
13. Various "turn-constructional units" are employed; e.g., turns can be projectedly one word long or they can be sentential in length.
14. Repair mechanisms exist for dealing with turn-taking error and violations; e.g., if two parties find themselves talking at the same time, one of them will stop prematurely, thus repairing the trouble. (700-701)

This system provides the framework for a wide variety of studies: how mothers and fathers talk to children, how men converse with women, how peoples of various cultures converse with one another. We can also examine how people speak to each other in classrooms, courtrooms, doctors' offices and welfare offices. As I read through this list, I am checking off items that seem to describe what happens when I conference and those that don't. Unfortunately, it seems clear to me that no matter how badly I want it to be, my conference talk at the moment is not really conversation. But I recognize instantly the voice of the classroom in my conferences.

The Language of Teaching

Language use in the classroom has been extensively studied for decades, first primarily in British classrooms where issues of class predominate in the research, and more recently in the United States, where the focus has been more broad, concerning itself with issues of gender, race, age, class, pedagogical style, and social reproduction. Studies of classroom talk indicate that it is radically asymmetrical. In the traditional teaching exchange, initiation of a topic is the teacher's right. Students are required to respond, and the teacher may or may not choose to evaluate that response or to supply feedback: a typical initiation-response-evaluation (or feedback) exchange, also called I-R-E or I-R-F (Sinclair and Coulthard, 1975). Michael Stubbs asserts that "teacher talk" is metacommunicative, constantly checking on the flow of information and language. Teacher talk is characterized by very particular functions: attracting and showing attention, controlling the amount of speech, checking or confirming understanding, summarizing, defining, editing, correcting, and specifying topics. He argues that "such a language is almost never used by pupils; and when it is, it is a sign that an atypical teaching situation has arisen" (Stubbs, 1983, 51-53). Stubbs draws on Labov and Fanshel's (1977) categorization of A, B, and A-B speech events to underscore the power of the teacher to control language—and knowledge—in the classroom. "A" events are those to which only the speaker has access, for they involve the speaker's (A's) emotions, experiences, and personal knowledge. Stubbs points out that "in school classrooms, a statement such as 'I don't know' may be the only one to which a pupil is not open to correction" (1983, 118). While we may not openly correct a student who says "I don't know," such statements certainly affect the shape of conferences, as I learned in looking at my own.

The difference between the forms and contexts of conversation and teaching is striking. The turn order in traditional teaching is fixed, as is, to some extent, the turn size. Discontinuous talk on the part of the student violates the expected I-R-E structure; if the teacher asks a question or initiates a topic, the student must respond. The work involved in constructing a conversation, on the other hand, is shared by all parties. While the structure of talk in teaching mirrors Freire's "banking concept" and indicates a hierarchy, conversation corresponds to the concept of collaborative learning Certainly, learning takes place in both collaborative and traditional teaching contexts, but in a classroom where the teacher talks and the student responds, where the teacher selects topics and students acquiesce, exploration and shared construction are not skills that students will learn.

Sociolinguistic Studies of Conferencing

There are researchers who hope for a productive pedagogical place for conferencing but who can see the problems with the contradictory accounts of conferencing that make up the bulk of work on the topic. Many are turning to the methods and questions that shape and drive sociolinguistics. Transcripts of conferences allow researchers to shift their focus from the revision of written texts to the structure of talk itself. Once that occurs, social relations are highlighted as well. Jacobs and Karliner (1977) for example, forward the

notion that conference talk "falls somewhere between classroom discourse and casual conversation and can draw its rules from either or
both depending on the styles of the participants and what they perceive to be the function of a particular conference" (503). Freedman
and Sperling (1985) also acknowledge the balancing act performed
by participants in conferences. A conference, they say, "has at least
the appearance of being spontaneous and personal behind its often
somewhat planned and pedagogic nature. Teacher and student must
operate at different levels—the conversational as well as the pedagogical—which may ultimately reinforce one another" (107-108).
Problematized versions of conferencing acknowledge the conflicting
paradigms and explore the ways in which participants negotiate the
conflicts. Irene Wong (1988), looking for a situation where "genuine
exchange" might result, analyzed conferences in technical writing
between tutors and tutees. Two tutees were graduate students in
engineering, and two were engineers, so all four brought a significant
knowledge base with them. Looking for what she defined as idealized
conference conversation—"discourse with a) balanced distribution
turns and turn size between the participants, involving b) an
exchange of information, in c) a context where both parties can
determine the agenda of the discussion" (450)—she finds it occurs
only 40% of the time and then when tutors respected the knowledge
bases of the tutees and elicited information from them relevant to
those knowledge bases. However, much of the time, tutors claimed
expertise even in those areas where they had little knowledge.
Speaking from the position of expert, they thus structured the talk in
traditional ways.

Melanie Sperling (1990) uses ethnographic and sociolinguistic
methodology to explore the collaborative nature of writing conferences in a ninth-grade classroom and the ways in which "participat-
ing in the explicit dialogue of teacher-student conversation, students
collaborate in the often implicit act of acquiring and developing
written language" (282). As she follows one white male teacher and
six students of varying gender, ethnicity, and levels of ability, she concludes that "as conferences move across tasks and time, patterns of
dominance tend to be tempered and teacher and student begin to
participate more equally, perhaps more collaboratively, in initiating
topics to discuss" (298). For Sperling, the form of conference talk and
the process of conferencing itself is "protean" and "shifting." In all
this, however, it is still the teacher whom

we often see engaging and sustaining the student's participation in writing conference conversation. The analysis, then, asks us to accommodate to the concept of a teacher-student collaboration what is seen here to be the teacher's special leadership role. That is, the analysis invites us to question commonly held assumptions regarding "ideal" conference interaction whereby the teacher, giving up decision-making power to the student, assumes a generally non-directive role. (295)

In such studies, we see the beginnings of an alternative, more complex description of conferences. Researchers do not assume that all students are equal, for example; rather, they consider particular aspects of students, such as gender, ability, preparation, etc. as important factors in shaping a conference. Freedman and Sperling, for example, examine whether high- achieving and low-achieving students elicit different responses from the same teacher during a conference. They conclude, after carefully examining transcripts from early semester "get acquainted" conferences, that high-achieving students elicited more praise, received more expository explanations delivered in a formal, "written-like" register of speech, and were offered more elaborate invitations to return for another conference. The researchers point out that the teacher in their study intended to treat all of her students equally; only when she could see through the transcripts how the conferences had been constructed by both her own and her students' talk did she realize what had occurred.

Ulichney and Watson-Gegeo (1985) describe teacherly control in their study of conference transcripts. Drawing on theories of social reproduction and constructionism, they examined conferences in two sixth-grade classrooms in which the teacher used a process approach to writing. What they discovered was that "pedagogical innovations, such as process writing approaches, may come to closely resemble familiar classroom routines as they are transformed by institutional pressures and familiar habits of schooling" (309). Ulichney and Watson-Gegeo used the analytic construct of the "dominant interpretive framework" or DIF, which they define as "the teacher's definition and interpretation of the ongoing situation and what counts for knowledge" (313). Students who successfully collaborated with the teacher and actively helped to construct her interpretive framework were positively assessed by the teacher. Even a student who resisted a correction offered by the teacher but was able to preserve the teacher's authority and dominance was evaluated as a "good" student. A student whose interpretation mismatched the teacher's, however, found herself confused at first, then silenced. Her personal knowledge was questioned and corrected, and she resisted with silence all further attempts by the teacher to draw her into the interpretive framework. The teacher's assessment of this last student was that she had an attitude problem, that she "can't write." Ulichney and Watson-Gegeo point out that average to low achieving working-class and immigrant students receive instruction

> that discourages initiative and expression. Literacy, especially being able to write effectively, means having a voice that reaches larger audiences and is preserved over time—a prerequisite for social empowerment. When education processes distribute that voice unevenly, they inadvertently perpetuate the inequalities of established power relationships between classes and society. When students resist the teacher's DIF, they may feel a sense of self-worth but they have effectively turned off what benefits school has to offer. (325-326)

Ulichney and Watson-Gegeo's research goes well beyond typical conferencing accounts. They are crucially concerned with the structure and outcomes of talk, not just written products that result from that talk. And they pay careful attention to the roles that students and teachers play in constructing conference talk.

How do we know that conferences are successful? The first and second generation conference descriptions remained vague on that subject; the usual criterion was, given the textual focus, that if the student's paper got better the conference had succeeded. But Carolyn Walker and David Elias (1987) analyzed student-teacher conferences rated as either very successful or unsuccessful by both teacher and student. Their purpose was to find out "who was doing what" and to describe the ways in which successful conferences differed from unsuccessful conferences. They concluded that in successful conferences, the focus was on the student and the student's work, with the teacher evaluating the work and both eliciting and articulating clearly the criteria for that evaluation. In low-rated conferences, however, there were a large number of questions and requests for explanations from both teachers and students: about the paper's content, about the student's writing process, and about the writing task. The focus of the conference remained on the teacher's expertise as a writer, with some teachers providing students whole paragraphs of the teacher's own words as part of the revising process. Finally, Walker and Elias hypothesize that time was spent on clarification of various kinds at the expense of time for evaluation and articulation of criteria, thus violating expectations of both parties that "evaluation should be the primary focus of the conference" (275). For Walker and Elias then, while a student's paper may have improved after a conference (sometimes because teachers rewrote them verbally!), that doesn't mean that students or other educators would find such a conference "successful."

What these more complex sociolinguistic studies of conferences show us is how great a leap we have made from the studies that focused on the logistics of conferencing, provided without explanation or support guidelines or questions for instructors to ask that would not be directive, and painted impressionist pictures of students and teachers working together that seemed more clear the further we got from the canvas. Research that has as its focus the structure and content of talk allows us to interrogate the kinds of broad statements and assumptions about conferencing that have been the heart of most literature on the subject and that grow from and reproduce the unexamined assumptions that shape our teaching and our culture. For example, Walker and Elias note that the common finding in most conference research prior to the publication of their own (1987) is that "students *like* conferences" (268). I cannot imagine that Felicia, a student in one of my conferences, liked the frustration I so obviously showed in speaking with her; I can't say I liked the conference with Dr. B. that sticks with me; my students have no difficulty remembering conferences they didn't like over the course of their academic experience. Like their teachers, they like the *concept* of conferencing. It is the practice that frustrates both teachers and students. For conferencing is not a genre of speech that we are familiar with; it is something that must be learned.

Conferences as Speech Genres

Murray points out that for his students to be successful in conferencing, they must learn how to ask the right questions. (Note that Murray assumes teachers already know the right questions to ask—a claim my own experiences call into question!) Sociolinguistic research indicates that conference talk is not quite the teacher talk Stubbs describes, nor is it conversation. For sociolinguists, the "context" created by speakers, speech, and situation—the context that is language, in Bruffee's terms—corresponds roughly to the concept of "speech genres." M.M. Bakhtin (1986) argues that speech genres are built on utterances, and utterances are intrinsically social, cultural, historic, and dialogic. For Bakhtin, an utterance is a unit of speech determined by a change in speaking subjects. In this way, it corresponds to what we usually consider a speaking turn. As such, it is inherently responsive; for Bakhtin, every utterance is a response to another utterance, is a "link in a chain of speech communion" (84).

> Any speaker is himself a respondent to a greater or lesser degree. He is not, after all, the first speaker, the one who disturbs the eternal silence of the universe. And he presupposes not only the existence of the language system he is using, but also the existence of preceding utterances—his own and others'—with which his given utterance enters into one kind of relation or another (builds on them, polemicizes with them, or simply presumes they are already known to the listener). Any utterance is a link in a very complexly organized chain of other utterances. (69)

It might be more appropriate to see utterances not just as a link in a chain, but as a link in a fabric of chain mail, connected historically and culturally—closely at times, more distantly at others—and always part of both an immediate situation and a larger context. Bakhtin writes of the "echoes and reverberations" of other utterances with the "communality" of the sphere of speech (91); these reverberations spread out in all directions, not just linearly.

Bakhtin's emphasis on responsiveness and the situatedness of participants in the community as speaking subjects differentiates his view of talk from the depictions of talk between students and teachers that we see in first and second generation accounts of conferencing. Bakhtin's metaphors evoke the kind of complexity of talk that is also missing from Bruffee, despite Bruffee's concept of the discourse community. For Bruffee, students belong to the same community simply because they are students. They are speaking subjects, but they are responding to the voice of a teacher and her peers, situated firmly in the classroom. He recognizes clearly the difference between teachers and students, but he is less clear on the differences among students. For Bakhtin, students would be responding not just to the immediate situation and the voices that are part of that, but to the "echoes and reverberations" of the respective communities of which they are a part, to histories of language that spin diverse narratives and offer multiple roles to each student. It was this din of voices that in part silenced me in Dr. B's office, that I tried to untangle in the relative shelter of a restroom, that complicate and enrich my life now.

The disciplinary presentations of conferencing as simply "student" and "teacher" become more problematic when we begin to consider not the two roles that we are usually presented with but the talk between people. When I conference with my students, then, each conference is linked to all conferences I have experienced or read about, and what I say is linked to things I have said earlier (for example, in previous conferences with the student or in class, or even to colleagues or at presentations or to myself!) as well as things that have been said to me. It is the same for the student.

Bakhtin argues that we are "given speech genres in almost the same way that we are given our native language" (78). Speech genres are "relatively stable thematic, compositional, and stylistic types of utterances" (64). Consider, for example, condolences we offer after a death, or "welcomes" to large events, eulogies, talk with strangers while in line, and so forth. We learn from practice, from those around us; we learn in a context that teaches us simultaneously language, role, and possibilities. We use speech genres to organize our relations with others in both simple and complex ways, from greeting one another to voicing disagreement to expressing love. Our ability to function competently in a variety of speech (and thus social) situations depends on our familiarity with the speech genres which correspond to those situations. If we wish to "speak freely" in a variety of situations, we must paradoxically understand the many forms of speech that are demanded by and create those situations, including conferencing. When we begin to consider conferencing as a speech genre, not simply as a practice almost inseparable from teaching, we have to ask ourselves how we learn it and how we can teach it effectively to our students.

What Happens When We Don't Know
Whether We Are Teaching or Conversing?

In conversation, we usually try to "match" our language to the language used by other speakers; it is part of the need to equalize the status of speakers, to minimize the "strain" that Bruffee points out. In my initial research on my own conferencing, I found myself doing just that. When students didn't use disciplinary language to describe their writing, neither did I. When students used it, I did, too. If I had conceived of the conference as a classroom, I would have said, "I'd like you to try to become more familiar with the terminology used by professional writers, critics, and teachers. So I'll use that terminology as I have in class and I'd like you to do so as well as we work our way through this paper. I'll define anything that I'm not sure is clear, or if you use a term in a way I'm not familiar with, I'll ask you to define it for me so that we're on the same wave length." Such a statement would be out of place in a conversation. Yet, if conferences are goal-driven—and I'd argue that the vast majority of them are—those goals have to be made explicit by both students and teachers. If we make those goals clear, however, we also make clear that we are not really "conversing," and the sense of equality and freedom that both students and teachers like about conferences fades away. When I didn't use the language I valued with students who didn't use it with me, it wasn't a conscious decision on my part. I was simply adjusting to a conversational partner and minimizing difference. I was also, in many ways, doing those students a great disservice by not acknowledging those differences, talking about what the effects of them might be as the student attempted to enter the academic community and making clear that one of my goals—perhaps not immediate, not for this conference—was to help the student learn that language. Critical theory, translated into practice, teaches students and their teachers about the power and social structure of the communities they are in or wish to enter and helps them make informed decisions about entrance, resistance, accommodation or affiliation.

Sometimes, digression on the part of a speaker may mean that she has wandered onto a familiar path that she feels bound to follow again, like the stories that Aunt Ellie tells each time she sees us. But often, digression is exploration, is learning: reconstructing experience and knowledge. We've found ourselves going somewhere we didn't expect. I have had students ask me for simple explanations of a small part of a text and found myself figuring out with them something I hadn't realized was even a question I had. I'm not sure that my digression, unreflected on or reframed to fit the genre, was much help to them, but it was to me. What about student "digressions?" Teacher-talk in part assures that such linguistic wandering will not take place in a classroom. But without a willing audience, the learning that might take place as the student moves into unfamiliar territory will not occur. When a student is willing to learn and the structure of conversation—her right to self-select as a speaker, to hold the floor as she thinks her way through a problem, her right to remain silent while she thinks and expect me to be silent while she is, to make a jump from one topic to the next without immediately explaining why—is overwhelmed by the teacher's perceived need to accomplish her goals using the language of the classroom to do so, then a valuable opportunity for active learning is lost.

It is difficult for talk that takes place in an institutional context involving a speaker deeply invested in that institution to break free of institutional restraints. So while the appearance of a conference may seem casual and conversational, beneath the surface is it often driven by the need for the teacher to cover whatever issues seem most pressing to her (particularly if she has initiated the conference) in the short time period most conferences occupy. If I am required to conference with my students a certain number of times and there are many more students after the one who is sitting with me at the moment, I am far less likely to respond personally to—if in fact I even hear—the fear and confusion in a student's words. If I do hear concerns deeper and more personal than the ones I have articulated or intend to, I may decide I don't have time to share my own experiences with her or ask more about her own, which, as a partner in conversation, I should. Or perhaps I choose not to make that time, foregrounding my role as teacher to any conversational role I could have chosen.

Juggling Talk, Encouraging Learning

What do your students expect from a conference? What do you? Is it an extension of the classroom, clearly tied to lessons learned there? Is it a place where students and teachers work to break down the kinds of institutional structures that both separate and bind them in classrooms and attempt to explore new relationships?

We teach students about poetry, short fiction, drama, and novels, but do we address in our classrooms the genres of speech that students need to be familiar with? Do we explore language as texts? If conferencing is a part of our practice, then we need to examine that part, teach that part, and reshape what happens if we don't like it, if it's not successful for both participants.

One way of addressing the conflict between conversation and teaching is to build into our curriculum an exploration of speech genres. Ask student teams to observe class members involved in conversation and note how it is structured, how topics are brought up and developed or dismissed, how feelings are dealt with, and how learning takes place. How do questions get asked and answered? How do turns shift? Was there a "point" to the talk? What function did it serve, what was accomplished, and how? Experiment with role playing: how would a team member talk about a personal problem with parents? A friend? A sibling? A pastor? A teacher? In a monologue? Have students monitor and break down classroom talk: lectures, mini-lessons, discussions, talk while the teacher is writing on the board or has his back turned, talk when a teacher responds privately to her student while writing is taking place (a mini-conference held in class), talk in peer or writing groups. Sacks et al. and Michael Stubbs offer clear lists of the features of conversation structure and teacher-talk; with these characteristics, students can place these genres they are exploring on a continuum of these features.

After such experience, students and teachers can determine what they want to happen in conferences. Frank discussion is needed to determine whether participants are uncomfortable when the talk becomes more personal, more conversational. What are the benefits of conversation for students? For teachers? What are the benefits of teaching? If students and teachers have identified learning taking place in conversations, can that same kind of learning be replicated in conferences? Should it be? If we were to place conferences on a continuum of talk, it might fall between teaching and conversation, and individual conferences may slide further in one direction or the other. As Bakhtin points out, "genres are diverse because they differ depending on the situation, social position, and personal interrelations of the participants in the communication" (79). When we cannot distinguish our conferencing from our teaching, we are often blind to the individual differences among students; when we are engaged in true conversation, the important goals of teaching may be ignored.

If we are open to conversation, we should pay careful attention to story-telling. It is a time-honored way of teaching, but it also makes up much of conversation. Deborah Shiffrin (1988) points out that telling a story takes time; therefore the usual pattern of turn-taking is suspended. The listener must release the floor and must adopt the speaker's perspective, becoming an audience. How rarely our students have teachers as an audience! What happens when teachers make room for both ways of storytelling? In the many conference tapes I've heard, extended stories were rare, but significant. One example comes from a conference between Mary, a teaching assistant, and Rick, a first-year student. They have struggled through an explication of Gerard Manley Hopkins' poem, "Spring and Fall," and Rick, obviously growing frustrated by what seems to him to be his stupidity, makes an awkward switch from a teaching segment to story-telling. Mary is open to what he offers. (For transcription notations, see Appendix B. Line numbers refer to original transcript.)

```
436 Mary:  Yeah. So I think that might be part of what he's
437         getting at here, that when you grieve you're always grieving for
438         yourself a little bit, huh?
439 Rick:                      ⌊See I might be- pl, I think we're alike in a lotta
440         ways cause we're both Catholic, an um..if I wasn't Catholic to
441         look at this maybe it'd be a totally different perspective.⌉
442 Mary:                              ⌊Mm-hmm           ⌊That's
443         interesting. Why do you think being Catholic makes a
444         difference?
445 Rick:  Well, you know, mourning an all that, you know, cause my
446 Mary:                          ⌊Mm-hmm
447 Rick:  parents are European so, whenever somebody dies, it's black for a
448         year an
449 Mary:  ⌊Big deal mournings, huh?
450 Rick:  Big funeral, you know⌈and if someone doesn't show up they
451 Mary:                      ⌊Uh-huh
452 Rick:  take offense to it, you know?
453 Mary:  A::h, wow. Wow.
454 Rick:  So, I mean.
455 Mary:  Yea:h, yea:h.
456 Rick:  Then you know you go tuh, uh..everybody shows up at the, you
457         know, funeral home an
458 Mary:  Yeah, yeah.
459 Rick:  So it's big you know
460 Mary:  Big deals, right.⌉
461 Rick:                  ⌊I know the first time I went, uh, a couple of
462         years ago, my great grandfather died, and it was just
463 Mary:  Blew you away, huh? (Rick makes a noise, Mary laughs.) You're
464         shaking your head there!
465 Rick:  I was up there n I was like (Mary gasps) you know, my mother
466         and my grandmother they're like, like an Dad, they've been to so
467         many it's just oh my God, it's like another thing for em, you
468         know, eh, we're goin to the funeral parlor tonight, okay.
469 Mary:  ⌊Right, right.                                    Get
```

470   dressed! (Laughs)
471 Rick: See you later! Have fun! See ya at nine! What are you doin,
472   you know? And I went out shaking, I couldn't stop shakin
             (turn continues).

Mary is clearly in control during the first two-thirds of this conference. Rick's earlier mention of his grandfather leads Mary to suggest that perhaps he might try a personal approach to the poem.
Suddenly, Rick changes the course of the conference, shifting into a
personal relationship with Mary, one based on shared religious perspectives, not on their student-teacher positions. Mary ignores
many opportunities to shift the talk back to the teaching structure
they had labored with before; in fact, this story-telling give and take
continues for another 43 turns! She supports his story by acknowledging she is listening ("backchanneling" words such as *Mm-hmm*,
Uh-huh and *Yeah*) and cooperatively overlaps her speech to support
him ("Big deal mournings, huh?"). Ultimately, Rick completes his
story not only about his great-grandfather's death but his grandfather's as well, including information about how his younger brother
wept without knowing why, while Rick himself grieved differently.
Mary points out that realizing that might well help him make good
sense of the poem. Had she not been open to this story, had she seen
Rick's attempt to shift the way in which the conference was being
shaped as an interruption of her teaching, rather than an opportunity for learning, he would not have had an opportunity to work his
way to a point where he might feel some control over the task ahead
of him in constructing his paper. And Mary would not have learned
about the ways that Rick's family and heritage shape his response to
course content and practice.

My own experiences have led me to begin tape-recording conferences with students. Students provide the tape and take it with them
when they leave. This allows us both to reflect on the conference further if we need to, and it has also changed something quite simple:
students no longer feel the need to take notes on their papers. Once
a student is taking notes, head bent down and attention on something other than the speaking partner, conferences quickly become
classrooms. The teacher's words become the law; students rarely
take notes on their own talk. If they are taking notes, they are
unlikely to initiate a story-telling segment; no one I know takes
notes during conversations and story-swapping. Taping conferences

has also allowed my students and I to track changes in conferencing patterns and to reflect on them at mid-semester and for the final course portfolios. What topics have resurfaced? What concerns have changed? What skills have developed?

If students like the concept of conferences, do they like actual conferences? How often do we ask them? Why don't we? What parts of the conference were most effective? What words did the teacher use that the student didn't understand? What questions did the student still have after the conference was over? What questions did the teacher have? Where did the conference seem to be working best? Why? What aspects of conferencing does each party want to work on for the next conference?

This kind of reflection and assessment can be built into course assignments and conferencing schedules. Leaving five minutes between conferences to jot down answers to these questions is all it takes. Students respond in writing and my practice is to keep a copy of that response in the file with their drafts and papers and remind students to review their response before the next conference so that we can prepare. A minute of review at the beginning of the conference helps us both remember what we wanted to work on or talk about.

When we focus on talk as well as written texts, we can track various kinds of successes and strategies. If a paper doesn't improve, student and teacher alike can search for a reason. It's common for teachers to talk about seeing the same paper a number of times; in all likelihood, they have also spoken to the same student a number of times. What did we say that helped improve this introduction? What have we said about this claim, that piece of support that hasn't seemed to affect the writing? How have we addressed or not addressed whatever fears, concerns, or problems that the student has that might have made all our teacherly advice about writing useless?

As teachers, we have to reassess what we "know" about conferencing. Have we absorbed an "ideal" conference structure from the materials we've read? What are the gaps in that picture? How have we filled them in with our own experiences? If we focus on talk and see all forms of communication as meaningful and purposeful, then can we categorize student talk as "digressive?" Or must we now see it as taking us down a different path from the one we prefer, but for a reason we need to understand? How does it change us—and are we open to and ready for that change—when we see students as *partners* in talk and learning? Real conversation demands partnership, and the benefits of real conversation may be radical and frightening. If a student sees the talk as conversation and reveals something personal about him or herself in a conference, we have fled conversation and retreated if we do not offer a similar personal revelation: in conversation, stories build on stories and revelations on revelations in the same way that lessons build on lessons in the classroom. If we reveal something personal, when we return to the classroom, we are vulnerable in ways that as teachers, we are not used to: our students know us in a new way. Yet students who work in teams over the course of the semester and gradually share information about themselves tell us over and over that such sharing, such trust, is what ultimately makes the team work. We become responsible for each other's revelations and stories, and that fosters an attitude that makes us responsible for each other's learning.

We need to examine, with our students, the myths of conferencing and the way those myths deny the power structures that usually exist. And we need to explore whether we want to make those myths into a reality and if so, how we shall be able to do that.

CHAPTER TWO

Power and Talk

MANY OF THE PROBLEMS THAT OCCUR BETWEEN STUDENTS AND teachers in conferencing arise because of the difference in power between participants. In classrooms, that power difference is indicated in many ways—for example, in the geography and use of physical space. In most classrooms, one teacher occupies the front third of the classroom, while in contrast, 20 or more students occupy the other two-thirds of the space. The teacher controls access to the chalkboard or overhead, and even controls how students will seat themselves. "Teacher talk" is also an indicator of power difference. It is very tempting, as we learned in the first chapter, to think that because the physical context has changed, because there are now just two "people" who "converse" about writing or literature, that everything has changed. Unfortunately, it takes a conscious effort on the parts of both participants to effect a significant change. Often, conferences are marked by silence on the part of students as teachers assert their perspective. Sometimes, students make it very easy for us to do that, even encourage teachers to tell them just what they need to know. Either way, it is the teacher's talk and the teacher's interpretation of a text that counts.

Drawing on the same theorists as Kenneth Bruffee, Peter Mortenson (1992) argues that talk is the negotiation of the social world that speakers inhabit together. Working from the notion of discourse communities, he states: "Since talk involves both consensus and conflict, to document this is to document negotiation of both consensus and conflict that constitute communities. These negotiations determine nothing less than who is allowed to say what to whom, when, how, and why—the social construction of texts" (120). Taking a broad view of what constitutes a "text," we can say that talk involves the reproduction or reconfiguration of social organization at both the micro and macro levels. And it is this tension between, on the one hand, the reproduction of social organization—teacher and student, male and female, Caucasian and African American—and the reconfiguration of it on the other hand—student and teacher as peers, fellow writers—that continues to provide both impetus and confusion to the study of conferencing.

These social relations are also power relations. Most of the conferences I hold with students are those I have initiated. I have the power to make students "come and see me" in the same way that I felt compelled to go see Dr. B. (And think about the use of the word "see!" Students are forewarned that they may be silenced!) I think we have to consider this fundamental power because it lies beneath much of the talk in conferences, particularly with first-year students. Students acknowledge that power by coming to conferences, even if they challenge it both subtly and openly, as I did in my conference with Dr. B. These power relations are also marked in language.

Who Gets to Talk?

One concern of critical discourse analysis is access to and participation in discursive events, particularly those events which have the power to affect lives in important ways. As Teun van Dijk points out, most people have very limited access to public discourse on important issues. They may discuss them at home or with neighbors, or perhaps participate in a demonstration, but they are not in the board rooms, at negotiating tables, in legislative sessions or budget meetings. In fact, he argues, most people have no preparation to speak in such situations and feel that it is in their best interest *not* to participate—an example of hegemonic control. We agree to let others speak for us. In many ways, this is also what occurs in traditional classroom settings. Teachers speak for all kinds of people, not just their students, and students accept that singular voice. Teachers reinterpret what students tell them, rephrase their words, select which ideas will be discussed and for how long. Most students accept this as natural, as do most teachers. It is a rare student who, like the student in Ulichney and Watson-Gegeo's study, steadily resists the dominant interpretative framework of the teacher, for the results can be institutionally and personally devastating. Who gets to speak in a conference? It is, in some ways, the "back room" of teaching, where advice is given, evaluations made, and decisions rendered that usually don't occur in the classroom. There is a great deal at stake for a student: don't speak enough, speak at the wrong time, talk too much, and you can be negatively evaluated. Say the "wrong thing," and there is nowhere to hide.

Consider how conferencing affects social identity and relationships. Imagine that an enormously important person gives a presentation at your institution. Many people listen to the lecture, but only a few have the "opportunity" afterward to speak briefly with the noted expert. Were I one of those people, I would speak about it afterward as a chance to "meet" with the speaker, to "talk" with the speaker, to "learn" from the speaker. To be honest, it's doubtful that I have learned anything more from our "talk" after the lecture than I did by hearing the lecture. What has changed, however, is my identity and my relationship to the issue or knowledge that was the focus of the lecture. I feel lucky or elite or awed or perhaps embarrassed at my inability to say anything "important," and I now have a "relationship" with someone important and so perhaps the sense that I have or could have a role in further constructing or reconstructing the world that person represents. Our students don't speak of "meeting" their teachers in the classroom, but they do "meet" for conferences. The social relationship has changed, and the opportunity exists for the student's relationship to the issue or the writing to change as well. Teachers and students are both aware of this change and the possibilities it offers—it's part of why we conference.

But how much of a role do students get in constructing knowledge? In actually shaping a conference? A word count in the fourteen conferences I examined after considering my own conferences indicates that, overwhelmingly, it is teachers who talk. (See Appendix C.) The conferences ranged in length from just under fifteen minutes to somewhere over thirty (in Don's conferences with students Lyn and Eva, the tape ran out near the end of the conference). Student participation ranges from a low of 2.3% for Lily as she speaks with her teacher, Nina, to a high of 40.2% for Rick, whose conference with his teacher, Mary, we've seen a part of already. Nina's conference with Lily is the shortest of all the conferences, only 1922 words (in comparison to Eric's conference with Dana, totally 6739 words). Lily spoke only 45 words, and almost all of those were to indicate acknowledgment or acceptance of the teacher's speech: *uh-huh, okay.* It's important to remember that both students and teachers found these conferences typical and successful. Yet, in sheer volume, talk is distributed in a radically uneven manner, one which falls clearly along the lines of status, generally reproducing in the conference the kind of teacher control that characterizes most classrooms. If what we are hoping for in a conference is genuine conversation, meaningful interaction, and a reshifting of traditional roles, we apparently will accept far less in lieu of that.

Marked Dominance

Consider some other markers of teacher dominance. Discourse markers help distinguish boundaries of talk (Schiffrin, 1988). For example, Rick and Mary discuss his developing understanding of a poem for a long stretch until Mary says: "So, that might be something you'd like to explore in the paper: what you learned about yourself." The *so* serves both to introduce a summary and to close a larger segment of speech. Stubbs (1983) demonstrates that markers allow us to predict not the syntax of the utterance which will follow it but the content. If, for example, I suggest a revision strategy to a student, and she begins her response with "Well," I will already (probably unconsciously, as marker knowledge and awareness are so deeply ingrained) be predicting that she is going to disagree with my suggestion or question it in some manner. Discourse markers, then, are ways of positioning a speaker either in relation to the information or another speaker, of responding to an earlier utterance, even of gaining the floor when speaking turns are contested. Returning to the example of the student who begins her response to my revision suggestion with "Well," I might interrupt her in anticipation of her rejection of the suggestion and begin a defense of it before she even gets a chance to offer her own. On the other hand, if she began her utterance with "I agree," I might be more likely to let her speak, even if she immediately followed her cue of apparent agreement with "but" and then made a counter suggestion. Discourse markers, then, are one important way in which we create coherence between units of talk, connect ideas, and shape the speech event at utterance, discourse, and even social levels.

Given the dominance of teachers in simple word count, it is no surprise that they dominate the talk in other ways as well (see Appendix D). Teachers use *and* in two powerful ways: to forcefully hold the floor and to string together ideas. *And* indicates that more speech is coming, and because of the difference in power between speakers, students are reluctant to claim the floor even if there is extended time after the *and*. Teachers used that time they had created to think ahead and ultimately to string together sometimes rather disconnected ideas into a narrative of knowledge, a story of learning that didn't always include the student. Teachers used *well* in the same way, to hold their place. But *well* is also frequently an indicator of disagreement or disjunction between request and response or marks a change in topic. Teachers' frequent use of *well* in these ways creates almost a constant opportunity to disagree or to delay answering a question. This is a powerful position to occupy—to not answer when someone makes a request or to openly prepare to disagree with a speaking partner. For some teachers, the other speaking partner sometimes appears to be themselves, the *well* referring to one of their own utterances that they now question. In this way, they are verbally constructing knowledge, which may be worthwhile for students to see modeled, but they are not constructing it cooperatively, with the student. And, significantly, *well* appears frequently in the conferences where knowledge and power are contested. Other markers—*so*, with its conclusive force; *but*, a contrastive; *you know* and *I mean*, with the relationships they forge between speakers and knowledge—all indicate the power teachers wield in speaking with students.

Webs and Narratives

Let's look closely at two conferences that show how two different teachers control and dominate their students in a conference, even when they mean well and are excited by the material they are dealing with. These teachers share the same goals: to improve their students' writing skills and their written work. But as the written work and the ideas that produce it are being reconstructed, the students are playing little role in the talk. In the excerpt below, Bill and Cari are discussing Cari's response to the novel *Beloved*. Bill speaks softly, slowly in conference. He reads the paper through first, then his usual strategy is to ask students what strengths they see in the work or what problems they would like some help with. Cari speaks clearly and with enthusiasm. This segment picks up not long into the conference.

209 Cari: That's what I was trying to decide as I wrote that.
210 Bill: Mm-hmm
211 Cari: What I was thinking.

212 Bill: I think that's a good way to write. I mean to write in ORDER to
213   figure out ⌜what it is that you wanna focus on. And then you
214 Cari: ⌞What I'm thinking
215 Bill: know, Cari, it's possible you could deal with both questions?... If
216   you think most readers if you think a lot of readers are gonna
217   have both questions in mind was she sane was she insane? Was
218   it an act of love? I don't know what the alternative would be
219   there, an act of anger? An act of selfishness?
220 Cari: Okay /⌜? /--
221 Bill: ⌞Uh that another thing you do touch upon whether it
222   was a selfish act or you and you say it's a selfless act.⌝
223 Cari: ⌞Mkay.
224 Bill: And see that in of itself (3 sec) is a really interesting is⌜sue.
225 Cari: ⌞Issue.⌝
226 Bill: ⌞I
227   guess the selfless selflessness and the love really fit together?
228 Cari: Mm-hmm⌝
229 Bill: ⌞Someone does something for you that's selfless you
230   you can usually say it's /on the basis/ of ⌜ove of some kind.⌝
231 Cari: ⌞Love   ⌞Yeah
232 Bill: Um (2.5 sec) but I still see two issues at work.
233 Cari: Okay.
234 Bill: And maybe you can deal with both of them or maybe you wanna
235   focus o⌜n one. It's gonna depend on what happens as we rework
236 Cari: ⌞On one.
237 Bill: it.
238 Cari: Okay.

Bill praises Cari's writing process in line 212 and clarifies that praise (*I mean*) immediately. He continues with a topic he introduced several turns previously, beginning his utterance with a coordinating marker (*and then*), although it is not linked to the praise it follows. Tagged immediately onto this coordinating link is a bid for a shared perspective, marked by *you know*. In line 214, Cari has attempted a cooperative overlap with Bill, predicting that he will praise her for writing to figure out what she is thinking, since she's told him already that was the purpose behind her writing. Bill, on the other hand, ignores what she's told him and praises her method of writing as a way of finding a focus, which seems to be a step ahead of where Cari envisions herself in the writing process. Disregarding the stage she indicates, Bill continues with his vision of how she can rewrite, reintroducing a topic he himself brought up several turns earlier. The *you know* in lines 213 and 215 asks Cari to share and accept Bill's version of the rewritten paper: he asks her to know as he does what the possibilities are for this paper. He works his way through the questions he would like her to address in her rewrite, and when she accepts (*Okay*) but goes on to say something else, he interrupts her to continue, reasserting and holding his place as speaker with *uh*. With the floor his, Bill returns to Cari's paper, using another *and* to tie the issue of selflessness to her text. Cari's backchannel (*Mkay*) is interesting. It is more indicative of accepting something given to her than of acknowledging or affirming the correctness of Bill's summary of her assertion. It may be that Bill has paraphrased her main point, and Cari is accepting the words of this paraphrase. Or perhaps Bill's paraphrase changes slightly Cari's point, and she accepts this version in place of her own.

Bill continues to hold the floor, beginning his next utterance with *and*. His directive *see* in line 224 once again asks Cari to share his vision, his opinion of what's interesting to explore and what isn't. He continues to work through his topic, holding his place with another *um* in line 232. The floor is so clearly his that Cari offers no topic or backchannel for 2.5 seconds (a long pause in talk!). Bill then problematizes the resolution he has tentatively reached and returns to his idea of dual topics, using yet another *and* to link what he "sees" to the strategies Cari can follow. He has created an ideal text that Cari can construct for him when she turns this paper in again.

In another example, Erin, a graduate assistant, and Jeff discuss in their conference Jeff's revision of a paper on Joyce Carol Oates's short story "Four Summers." Erin speaks quickly and energetically.

303 Erin: Let's see. Um, I think maybe I would just move this second
304   paragraph then somewhere towards the end.
305 Jeff: Okay.
306 Erin: And, you talk about, in in the end of your introduction you talk
307   about (reading) "I believe that nothing will change in Sissy's life
308   when her child is born." And I might go straight into this, I can't
309   blame Sissy for wanting her life to be different. And explain
310   why, uh, you talked about how you feel sympathy for Sissy in
311   your introduction, you talked about how um, nothing will
312   change. You can start setting your reader up then, by: sketching
313   out like you do here that, that (2 sec) the empathy you feel for
314   her, and you can't blame her for wanting her life to be different
315   and then sketching it out a little bit in the questions you ask.
316 Jeff: ⌊Okay.

Erin's use of *and* not only controls the amount of speech Jeff can contribute but sets up a powerful narrative of revision. Each step is linked equally to the one before and the one that follows. Further, although it is difficult to tell from this brief excerpt, Erin's views on this story are becoming part of this narrative of revision. The "you" in line 314 is just as much Erin's larger "you-as-anyone" as it is a paraphrase of Jeff's text. Near the end of the conference, this blending of the teacher's voice and the author's voice is again made clear, when Erin says: "I don't- it's not that simple, that's that's my whole message that's Oates' whole message in this story."

There is a sense in these conferences that teachers are a part of a powerful narrative. Their use of *and* is pervasive, integral to their speech. It connects disparate ideas in ways that iron out seams and close possible ruptures where another voice, another narrative might be inserted like rib-splitters. Notice, for example, how in the excerpt below—also from Erin and Jeff—Erin uses *and* to connect what she presents as fact to what she presents as personal opinion.

```
390 Erin:                    Um (5 sec) so you might
391        want to complicate that a little bit and and talk about how (3 sec)
392        social class isn't isn't a biological given, uh, social class is
393        socially constructed for reasons, um
394        (16 sec, reading?)
395 Erin:  And I like your ending a lot better this doesn't sound that kind
396        Miss America-ish stuff that
397 Jeff:  Yeah
398 Erin:  You know.
```

The *and* in line 395, after a 16-second pause in which she shifts topics, indicates that Erin sees larger connections between her utterances—some kind of structure external to the conference itself—than any microanalysis of a few exchanges will demonstrate. It is a dynamic structure, like a spider's web, sensitive to whatever touches it, changing its shape in subtle ways—responding to damage, new opportunities for stronger connections—and repeating itself again and again from one instance of creation or evocation to the next. We recognize it as much by its purpose—to catch and hold—as by its structure. A fly becomes entangled in a web and the spider begins to wrap strand after strand of silk around it. Soon, the fly is connected to all parts of the web, and though no less a fly than when it first entered the web, it is now also something else. The spider depends upon holding that fly, keeping it entrapped, making it a part of the larger structure. And while certainly teachers don't feed off their students in the same way that spiders do off flies, we depend upon them and have as much at stake in making them a part of our web. Unlike the fly, the student will walk away, but once part of that web, we believe they will never *not* be connected again.

The strands are the language of the discipline, the particular structure of our knowledge. Erin tells Jeff: "Um: (3 sec) I'm not really sure how to tell you how to do this without giving you.. my sentences, but let's see." Later, she checks with him: "Now does that make sense? I've done more talking than you have, but um, I can see the paper taking shape." Jeff assures her it makes sense.

A conference is a web of ideas, beliefs, and values—a community shaped by its language and the knowledge it holds to be truth. Teun van Dijk (1993) points out that most effective power is cognitive, not physical; the power elite set out to change the minds of others in their own interests. Such change may not be openly manipulative but very subtle, part of the "naturalizing" process that makes inequality of power appear "right." Look at the weight of *you know*s and *I mean*s as teachers speak to students, creating and reshaping that community, defining it for a possible member. While *you know* can focus attention on upcoming speech (for example, "You know, I never thought about that until now, but..."), it can also mark shared knowledge, subtly forcing another speaker into a cognitive relationship that becomes a linguistic relationship that marks and cements the social relationship. If the penalties are too great for challenging that shared knowledge (it's a rare student who could or would say, "No, I don't know. What ARE you talking about?") and the options for other responses are slender, then we shape by force. The basic power structure remains untouched, for even as a teacher's *you know* forces a student into at least appearing to assent to shared assumptions, the use of *I mean* acknowledges the lack of shared knowledge, the teacher's ability to construct and reconstruct knowledge as the student struggles to follow. Eric, a full professor, and Dana discuss Dana's paper on *Jane Eyre*. Dana is lost throughout much of this portion of the conference, and yet knows that she must "get it."

347 Eric: You know, one way of letting people go is to identify yourself
348   with them.

349 Dana: That's a good point, I I yeah. I mean I didn't, I mean I I can
350   usually see what you're saying but I mean that's not something
351   that I, I don't, I was thinking I I could see what you're saying
352   about um Bessie was with her she was somewhat that way with
353   Adele
354 Eric: Yup
355 Dana: I I thought of that but, I mean obviously I didn't put it in the
356   paper but, I guess, I hadn't thought about um, let's see, how in,
357   I mean, you know what I'm sayin? / ? /--

Eric interrrupts Dana here to clarify the point he tells her she has made. She is obviously struggling to understand what Eric sees almost happening in her paper; she is unable to yet articulate his ideas. Finally, Dana summarizes Eric's argument, not as a concept she now understands and has considered, but as a point she must make in order to be positively evaluated by her instructor.

387 Dana: So you're
388   just sa- saying that it would have been, it would have been
389   beneficial if I had ju- I had gone to say that, I mean exactly what
390   you said, that that Jane internalized each of these three women and
391   and each of them contributed to her character ⌈n that--
392 Eric: ⌊Yeah I think that's
393   implicit in this paper and I would have gone on to make it
394 Dana: ⌊Mm-hmm
395 Eric: explicit.
396 Dana: Nkay. Awright. I can see that.

Dana's use of the word "beneficial" underscores the power relationship that helps shape this conference. It's an odd word to use when discussing the revision of a paper, unless the speaker is more concerned with the grade than the text. In order to be the beneficiary of Eric's grade, which will be left to her in a grade report, Dana must make use of another of Eric's legacies: his words. She must say, as she notes, "exactly what [he] said."

Cooperation

One of the assumptions of critical discourse analysis is that there is rarely a clear-cut line between the dominated and the dominating: van Dijk (1993) argues that "one major function of dominant discourse is precisely to manufacture...consensus, acceptance, and legitimacy of dominance" (255, citing Herman and Chomsky, 1988). The control Bill exercises over Cari's access to the floor in the excerpt a few pages ago is not—with the exception of his interruption in line 221—heavy-handed. Rather, it is with Cari's support. There are four cooperative overlaps in this one segment and three instances of backchanneling—agreement or support either latched onto Bill's utterance or positioned during normal pauses. It is a rare case in these conferences where the teacher overtly forces an interpretation on a student. Rather, the student agrees without any explicit urging to the teacher's interpretation.

That gray zone between force and cooperation is apparent in the following excerpt. We shape by cooperation—and force—when we follow a strategy of creating the "other" and then marginalizing that other. As Erin argues for a particular perspective in her conference with Jeff, she sets up two communities: those who agree with her and those who don't.

```
141 Erin:   (Continuing turn)         What
142         I'd like to see you do in the introduction, um (4 sec) is talk a little
143         bit about why you think you might be sympathetic toward Sissy
144         and others in the class were complete opposed to her? I mean,
145         wh why do you think your response as a reader was on one side
146         when clearly half the class was for the other, from the other
147 Jeff:                  ⌊Okay
148 Erin:   side. You know, we heard the arguments, well, my parents, uh,
149         have always told me I could be anything I wanted to be, an you
150 Jeff:                                                      ⌊Yeah
151 Erin:   know, Sissy should just go, have gone straight to college instead of..
152         getting married and having babies, and th that's.. I think that's
153         a superficial reading of the short story.
154 Jeff:   I think it's like, well, the person himself / ? / say that. Like the
155         people that say like it's your own fault, they're shal- you know,
156         people like that are kinda almost shallow because they don't see
157         that other people are have problems like this because they never
158         did.
159 Erin:   Well, and they're kind of, that's the kind of the point I've been
160         making all semester, the the situation you're born into has a
161         whole lot to say about how far you go in a society and there's
162 Jeff:                                                        ⌊Right
163 Erin:   sometimes there are certain circumstances you can't overcome.
164         Now I'm not arguing that Sissy couldn't have had a different
165         life. What I'm trying to get people to realize is that in Oates'
166         short story, she points out certain aspects certain people in the
```

167   society that just- (3 sec) we aren't all born with the same
168   chance..⌈of success, and I think that's what Oates is saying or at
169 Jeff: ⌊Right
170 Erin: least I think she wants you to consider that. Now you don't
171   have to agree with th⌈is and half the people don't have to agree
172 Jeff: ⌊No, I do
173 Erin: with that but what the I DO ask them to do is examine that..
174   statement ⌈that that Oates is making. You could have written this
175 Jeff: ⌊Right
176 Erin: paper from the other side and and and looked at Oate⌈s's
177 Jeff: ⌊Right
178 Erin: argument and said well, you know, Sissy was incredibly / ? /
179   you know, I would have a hard time arguing that side but I'm
180   not saying it can't be done.
181 Jeff: Mm⌈-hmm
182 Erin: ⌊Because I happen to be sympathetic toward Sissy's plight.

Erin disagrees with a particular reading of "Four Summers" and labels it "superficial." Jeff, wishing to distinguish himself from the half of the class who shared that reading, picks up on Erin's derogatory term and develops it. At first it appears that he will label those "other" students as shallow, but he stops himself, marks that he is merely sharing Erin's description (*you know*), and then hedges his description: "kinda almost shallow." Jeff is walking a tightrope. He is speaking of his friends and classmates, yet a lot hinges on his marginalization of them. Erin hedges her response, beginning with a marker of disagreement, but following it with a coordinating marker as she adds to Jeff's description. But she shifts instead from derogating these particular students to the point she says she has been making "all semester" to the class. Her emphasis on "all semester" is another, subtle way of marginalizing that half of the class: they either have not understood her repeated point or have chosen to challenge it. Either characterization is negative. No wonder Jeff rushes to assert his agreement with her point of view in line 172. Erin, perhaps realizing what she has done, offers the idea that really, it doesn't matter what you argue as long as you do it well, but she immediately undercuts that by saying she would have a hard time arguing the point these others want to make. (And if the teacher has difficulty, where does that leave the students?) Notice the change in Jeff's responses to Erin. They begin with a noncommittal *okay* and *yeah* but shift to actual support: "Right" he says repeatedly.

In a similar vein, Don, a teaching assistant, tells Lyn that he assumes that students learn mechanics, punctuation, and syntax in high school, and that some of his students' papers "get so bogged down with bad writing and fractured syntax that…I just sorta throw the paper down, I can't read that shit." Lyn laughs with him, for of course, since he told her this so conversationally, it can't mean her. But what if it does? She can't sort out where she stands with him and these bad writers, so she suggests that her paper might be one of those, checking on her status in the class. Lyn accepts—at least on the surface—Don's assumptions about learning and even the way he says he responds to violations of his expectations. But it's a frightening thing to accept. If much of the way we connect to our students is through their writing and that writing is "shit" to be thrown down and ignored, what does that say for our relationship with students?

As Mina Shaughnessey (1977) points out, unless conventions are discussed and understood, many students will simply attempt to integrate all of them, producing writing that is confusing to readers. For example, Dana explains to Eric that she used commas around an *and* in her paper because she had learned in high school that no more than one *and* per sentence was allowable. But imitating the more complex syntax she was seeing in college, she'd used more than one *and*. She then applied a rule that setting a piece of text off with commas meant that it could be lifted out of the sentence—that it was, essentially, parenthetical. She explained that she'd used commas as she had to make it clear to Eric that this wasn't the real *and*. Eric is unique in asking why Dana chose to use commas oddly, but his dismissal of high school writing conventions is not. Over and over in these conferences, students are informed of the conventions of college writing, not just conventional readings of literature but conventions of form and position. Nina posits for Lily and Kate readers who will be upset if citations and non-sexist language aren't used appropriately, clearly a community much like herself. Bill tells Cari that to prove you know your text, you must quote from it. (To prove to whom? That you "know" it how?) Carl explains to Dave that in a model essay exam, the answer is "laid out" for the teacher, so that he doesn't have to search through the writing to find it. Nina tells Kate to "watch things like absolute statements." It's like telling a student to "watch out for speeding cars." There is something awfully threatening about this learning.

I don't wish to argue that these rules and conventions are right or wrong, useful or trivial—I can see them as being helpful within this community. My concern is whether the uncritical presentation, enforcement, or acceptance of them results in a form of oppression, inequality, or marginalization. When we accept a rule as "right" or "good," when a convention is "just what is done," then we have set off a whole group of words or thoughts that are "not right." Thoughts that are not spoken, knowledge that does not count, acts that cannot be committed. And students who have not mastered the conventions are silenced, their papers lying in the pile of bad writing that a teacher can no longer bring himself to read. This is not just an academic game; the results are real. Consider the fate of the young student in Ulichney and Watson-Gegeo's study who challenged the teacher: she was labeled a "bad writer" and spent the year in silence. Consider Jeff's new relationship with his classmates, the difficulty of working with and respecting them in peer groups—the difficulty of respecting himself and his teacher—after derogating them in private during his conference. The desire to join this powerful community is powerful. Dana is upset and confused by her grades in a literature class with a teacher other than Eric, for in the past, she thought she was "pretty good at it." She can't even approach this teacher, for she doesn't know what to say. She tells Eric haltingly: "I just, I wish there was something.. I don't, I don't have a real specific question that I can just go up and ask him, I just, I just wanna say, tell me what to look for in the work that makes me BE insightful." Whatever it is she is seeing is not "insightful" enough. She wants not just his grade, but as the transcript shows, she wants to be a part of a community of students and teacher that IS insightful, prestigious, powerful.

Summary

Control of conference talk takes place at a number of levels. Teachers talk more than their students, and they hold on to their speaking rights not only through the power that their roles as teachers accord them, but by structuring the spoken text to create a powerful narrative. Instructors often seem to be speaking not just to their students, but to a larger audience, to other voices beyond the conference. Beyond the structural level, teachers use relational markers such as *you know* and *I mean* to invite or evoke the concept of shared knowledge and of the student's entry into the community represented by the teacher. Simultaneously, they reinforce the status differences by complicating and reformulating the very information they just agreed upon as shared, marking their ability to complicate (or clarify, depending upon where you sit) with *I mean*. Finally, teachers sometimes replace the conventions and rules that students bring with them from an earlier community, but more often they simply add those appropriate to college English, to their own academic community, thus controlling not only talk about texts but the students' written texts as well. And they usually do this without any interrogation of custom and without discussion of the contextual nature of conventions.

As teachers speak in such a way and students listen and accept, together they build up what van Dijk calls "preferred models" of discourse, of social relations, of knowledge. In these conferences the preferred form of discourse is linear, relationships are heirarchical, and knowledge, though not always reified and given, is also not negotiable. Those who demonstrate understanding and acceptance of this model will find in return praise and acceptance; those who do not understand or challenge this model will become the "half of the class" Erin marks so clearly as "other."

In the real time of conferencing, we may sense that this isn't the close conversation we wanted, but at least we have an interested audience and a bit of give and a lot of take with a student. And so we often settle for that, hoping that at least someone learned something, and we move on. The written product may be better, ultimately, but whether the student is a better writer is debatable. And the student, impressed that the teacher took the time to talk with her and considered her paper so thoroughly, leaves feeling like she was given a lot of information to help her improve—now if only she could understand it or remember all of it! Why is she so dumb? She looks at her paper later that day, maybe a few days or even weeks later, depending upon the class structure, and what returns? How much will she remember when she has played so passive a role? When she has all sorts of new conventions that she will simply add into the stock of conventions she brought with her that have not been examined or discussed? She turns in the paper, revised, and we shake our heads and wonder why it has changed so little or has become so odd or confused.

Reconsidering Power and Status in Conferencing

The teachers in this study—like teachers who are my current colleagues and friends, like myself—did not go into conferences intend-
ing to dominate and control. They did not think that they would shut
out a student's perspective. I have often felt, like them, that somehow,
my power as a teacher would melt away miraculously when I sat
down alone with a student. It is easy for me to forget that what I am
saying to a student is part of Bakhtin's "chain of utterances," that the
student has a history of teachers and teachers saying certain things
and that whatever I say becomes by default a part of that chain, is
seen in the context of that history. That chain of utterances seems to
have injured more people than I can count. Probably most of us who
teach writing have had strangers back off from us physically when we
tell them what we teach and exclaim nervously: "Writing was my
worst subject!" I remember a time when I was lying on a table in an
emergency room getting my face stitched up, and the young woman
doing this delicate work backed away in horror as I told her I taught
writing. Curved needle in her hand, in control of my recovery and
my appearance, still she stammered in fear and memory of humiliation that she didn't speak well. It is this power, where even if I have
no history with a student, she brings one with her and attaches it to
me, that invades conferences. Students make it easy for teachers to
dominate conference talk; they encourage it in many ways.

If the asymmetry of conferences is going to shift, the asymmetry
of the classroom must shift as well. If a goal of teaching is to
"empower students" then how are our classrooms empowering? If
they are not, then it will certainly be difficult for our conferences to
be empowering. A critical review of classroom practice, implementing change after that reflection and continuing to examine our practice critically, will make any disjunction or connections between
teaching and conferencing practice clear.

When I first began teaching, the power of it all frightened me. So I
grabbed onto some techniques offered in a pre-teaching seminar, not
to empower students but to avoid empowering myself! I had students
sit in a circle. I used portfolios not for all the skills and abilities they
help students develop, but because I could put off final grades that
way. I didn't even give grades until midsemester because I wasn't sure
I could grade well enough. I told students to put themselves into
groups large enough to give good feedback and small enough to get

work done in the time we had. I didn't assign topics. I didn't know if there was chalk at the blackboard because I'd never been up there.

Some wonderful things happened. Students didn't ask for grades but told me they liked how I responded on tape and talked like a real reader, not a teacher defending a grade. Some groups were three students, some were two, some were four. Group members switched around sometimes to get new readers. They gave each other topic ideas. Dutiful readers told me which chapters of the university-required book were good and told other students what to read and what not to read and why—and offered good reasons for their decisions to do or not do the work. Students told me what they needed to work on, what scared them, what they wanted to get out of the class. They worked toward those informal goals. They loved the course and I remembered how much fun learning could be. Wow! What a great class! I felt so good about myself and my students, I decided I was ready to become a teacher!

So over time, I became comfortable with assigning topics, giving grades, organizing groups, writing a syllabus that laid out the semester's work in relation to the goals I had set. I got a lot of praise from teaching mentors and institutions for what I now realize was extensive control over most aspects of the classroom: structure, talk, learning. I wanted to empower my students, too. I was convinced that the way to do it was to teach them to speak, think, and act in a way that was institutionally sanctioned, for after all, my power and prestige had grown as I'd "learned the ropes" of college. There was so much to learn, so far for them to travel that I didn't have time to explain it all, and if I did stop to explain something, I didn't question it. My students didn't see anything wrong with my teaching; it was just like most of their teachers. She really cares about us, they said, she wants us to be successful.

When I began examining my conferencing, when I studied in a critical framework the way I had structured the talk and set up the outcomes, I wanted to change how I conferenced, and I had to go back to the classroom to make changes there as well. So—my students sat in a circle for large discussion. Big deal. Who decided what was going to be discussed? So—my students worked in groups and could revise all semester. I decided who would be in those groups, I set up the guidelines for working in them, I set the tasks, and I evaluated the talk. They picked their topics, but I was really the only reader that counted. What I liked and didn't like about each essay was paramount. I remember how a student translated my taped comment on a paragraph. I had told her that it had some problems in organization; she wrote next to it: "Teacher hates this part. Bag the whole thing."

What opportunities for real power do we create for students when we construct our classroom? What substantial decisions do they get to make? How much class time do we allot for discussion of student goals? How much flexibility do we build into a course to value those goals by accommodating them?

Changing practice is the topic of many books; in this small portion of a chapter, I can only make some suggestions for beginning to form a learning community where power is less asymmetrical. In many cases, I can offer questions that help in restructuring a class; the activities that answering such questions generate are myriad. In chapter one, I suggested that students and teachers study language together, that they consider the way that conversation and teaching differ and what it means for social relations. In the same way, the structure of the classroom and learning can be studied. Students can begin with definitions and categories of teachers and learners. We can do the same. We cannot erase the history that students bring with them of traditional classrooms any more than we can erase our own. But since we all categorize and define, we can examine what we put into particular categories and why—by we, I mean both teachers and students. For example, if I hear a colleague say about another colleague: "Oh, she told me how she was using that book in her class, and she is so retro!", I would probably ask for some more details in order to determine what her definition of "retro" is for the teaching of literature. (Not just because I'm interested in assessment and evaluation, but because I'd want to determine whether I'm retro, too!) My guess is that if teachers were to examine what they thought a "good" student was, they would find some conflicts: followed some rules but challenged or broke others? Thinks for self but accepts teacher's ideas eventually?

Discussion of these definitions and categories can be enlightening, a little disheartening, and exciting if we take them seriously. What assumptions need further examination? Where did we get these categories and definitions? How have they shaped us? Where does the teacher fit in? Where does each student fit in? What does that mean in terms of change? Students can bring in copies of syllabi from their various classes and examine them to determine what definitions of learning, teaching, and social relations are assumed by various professors. Your own syllabus is equally fair game for analysis.

What goals do your students have for their writing? For this class? How did they generate those? What goals do you have? Where do these goals match? Why? Where do they differ? I speak frankly with my students about some of the ways the institution I am a part of shapes my goals. Such discussion has made me realize where I have more power and discretion than I thought and has helped me understand the reasoning behind some of the guidelines that inform my courses. For example, if I am required to use a particular text, I tell them that. But does that mean that I must use all of it? That they can't select sections to read themselves that connect to their goals? And why *this* text? How long ago was this set in stone? Can we begin a process of change?

When I accept that my students may have better ideas than I about how to reach my goals, then power begins to shift. And if I accept that their goals may be as valid as mine, then power continues to shift. Negotiation of goals means changing the structure of the course. It is empowering for students to help determine in substantial ways what will happen in a course. In most traditional classrooms, teachers don't have to justify why they use writing groups, or why they've chosen a text—basically, they don't have to justify anything about their practice, at least to their students. But when it is all up for discussion and "because I think it's best for you" no longer carries much weight, power shifts. In a community of learners, does it matter how you reach a goal? Whose idea it is? Yes and no. If all the "learners" were equal in status to start with, no. But if some of the learners are suddenly more powerful, have a higher status than before, have the opportunity to be truly active in learning, yes. It is empowering to be taken seriously.

Students learn quickly that sharing power means sharing responsibility. If students decide how writing groups will be organized—and maybe after trying them decide whether they want to continue with them—then they also are partly responsible for how well they work. As a member of that learning community, I have a responsibility to share with them any knowledge I have that will help them achieve their goals, but also to contextualize thoroughly that telling. What happens in such a classroom is that there is never just one way to do something or a "right" way of thinking, writing, or speaking. Instead, options open up constantly and decision-making and critical thinking become a crucial part of learning. What constitutes "good" writing from their past experiences? What constitutes it now?

What does that say about the two communities that evaluate writing? This leads, almost inevitably, to discussions of Shakespeare and Stephen King, greeting card verses and T.S. Eliot, student evaluation of student texts and teacher evaluation of the same texts. "My group said it was great but the teacher trashed it!" What standards can we not let go of as teachers? Why? What standards that our students hold should we consider seriously? Regular reflection on the class structure and readjustment of the syllabus and activities keeps everyone responsible for learning.

I use a portfolio now not because it allows me to put off grading but because it can afford students so much control over their writing. As a class, we discuss the portfolio throughout the semester as a working portfolio: students reflect on how their writing has changed, what they've learned, how they learned it, how it connects to their initial goals, and how their goals may have changed as they've written and read classmates' writing. Near the end of the semester, as a class we decide how much the final course portfolio should be worth in the course grade each student receives, and how much each of the other course activities should count. I do not assign specific values to them initially, for in one class, presentations may be more valuable than journals, in another, students feel that participation should count more than presentations. As a teacher, this is one of the most exciting class meetings I experience, as I listen to students talking with each other about the relative value of all the work they've done this semester, regardless of any grades they have received. I participate, too, but my voice by this time in the semester doesn't carry as much weight as most other teachers expect. Students and I decide what should, at a minimum, be in the portfolio and how much they can individualize it. By then we have read sample portfolios and discussed them and the reading and grading process, and so, like the decisions they make throughout the semester, their choices in constructing their portfolios are informed by experience, discussion, and an understanding of contexts and communities outside our own.

How does all this translate into a difference in conferencing? In the taped conferences I examined, students had constructed responses to texts that were, it seemed, inevitably challenged. Challenge is not necessarily a bad thing. But usually the teacher offered his or her own interpretation, without a great deal of support for that reading; it was simply a better reading because it was the teacher's. And over the course of the conference, teachers often tried to replace the student text with their own. Sometimes students resisted, sometimes they eagerly accepted the teacher's text. In a classroom where something as apparently innocuous as a syllabus can be examined critically and the teacher must support or reconsider the text in light of student arguments and questions, it becomes difficult for the same students and teachers to sit down one-to-one and change that pattern. Students informed about the patterns and social relations assumed by conversational and teacher talk, students used to making substantial decisions and being responsible for their learning are less likely to accept without question a teacher's interpretation of a text. They are more likely to offer extensive support for the organization of a paper. They are better able to hold the floor in the conference because they have held the floor in the classroom and in significant group work. The structure of the critically informed classroom has been changing what feels "right" and "natural" to students and teachers. Something closer to equality has been replacing the asymmetry of more traditional classrooms. If we move back toward that asymmetry after such radical change, it may feel right and familiar (most of us have been participants in that asymmetry for a long time!) or it may feel suddenly very wrong. Either way, we will notice that disjunction as much as our students, and awareness is crucial for change.

When I studied my own conferences, I wondered at the way that students who worked effectively in peer groups, often in leadership roles, suddenly became silent or tentative in a conference. When I examined my classroom practice, I realized that substantial leadership was only possible when they were working with peers; in all other class forums, I retained power and leadership. There was only one teacher but many learners. So in conference with me, students who had been "teachers" in their peer groups abdicated that role; I was the one true teacher and they felt they could not usurp even the smallest part of that role. It didn't matter that I spoke personally, that I urged them to talk, that I created the surface appearance of conversation; they responded to the structure of the classroom and felt those same supporting structures beneath the casual surface of the conference. It is important, then, that in the classroom, there are also chances to interact with the teacher—not just peers—in ways that do not reproduce the traditional roles.

In chapter one, I urged teachers to think about speaking with student as partners, for when we speak with peers and partners, we value what they say, we listen to the substance of their ideas, and we encourage verbal give and take. When we speak to colleagues about literary readings, we don't run over their ideas with a steamroller of words; instead, we listen to their interpretations, ask questions to help us understand their perspectives, and offer our own. When we compare that kind of talk, that kind of "conference" (why is it we "conference" with students but "discuss" with peers?) to what occurs between teachers and students, we begin to get a sense of what kinds of changes need to occur in our classrooms if we are going to change our conferencing.

CHAPTER THREE

Gender and Conferencing

RECENTLY, A GROUP OF STUDENTS IN MY FIRST-YEAR COMPOSITION class ran a game in which three teams competed for a prize of candy by correctly answering questions about grammar. Members of each team signaled their readiness to answer by shouting "Bing!" There was no penalty for a wrong answer except that another team could then try. I realized, as I watched a team of all women competing against a team of mostly men, that the women, all of whom I knew to be very competent students, rarely shouted out "Bing!", while their male counterparts shouted it immediately after the question had been asked, even if they didn't know the answer to the question. The female team came in last. Why, I wondered, were they so reluctant? Being wrong had no penalty. Why did they wait until they were positive they were right? It took me awhile to rethink the question. What other kinds of penalties or losses would they suffer if they shouted out? If they were wrong? What was there to gain? Was candy enough? What risks did this game have for them that I had not considered?

It was a simple game. I hadn't predicted this response when the students ran it past me for advice. But conferencing is supposed to be simple, too. As I'll discuss later, there *are* penalties for women who shout out in class, and after years of schooling, we have learned them well. And winning? There is a dark side to that for women as well. As the presenting group members exhorted the women to try harder, I thought about how hard they might be trying already—to meet one or another contradictory expectation.

In none of the conferencing studies we considered here—including those that use sociolinguistics—has the issue of gender been more than a matter of a "variable" if it has been considered at all.

Why not? The tensions between conversation and teacher-talk that we've examined in the first two chapters aren't merely about the structure of language or academic hierarchy; they are tensions about the structure of knowledge, of power, of access to learning and authority. Studies that examine the content and structure of conferences without considering the location from which the participants speak appear to accept the neutrality of language and the myth of the classroom as a great equalizer. We all want to believe that we treat our students equally, regardless of their class, race, age, gender, or other characteristics, regardless of our own. After all, we've been educated out of those prejudices by our participation in classrooms where we've been given "the truth," where we've read widely, where we've come into contact with all kinds of people. Our students also accept the idea that classrooms are neutral spaces, for at the slightest sniff of some perceived inequity there is an outburst of anger. It is as if teacher and students meet to speak and learn free of the effects of their lives, their gender, their race, even somehow free of the language they use and value, free of the kinds of academic patterning that results from years of participation in an institution dedicated as much to socializing as "educating."

I remember re-reading the transcripts of my own conferences and being struck by how tentative the women were in speaking with me, how confident the two white males were. I realized that even as I was reading I was feeling that the female tentativeness meant those students weren't going to be able to revise their papers, that they needed more help and that even if I gave them that help, they wouldn't know what to do with it. I believe some of those assumptions came from what was almost a refrain in the conferences with women—over and over, they said "I don't know." They used the phrase to refer to their ideas, to my direct questions, to their developing interpretations of the literature we were reading, and to their plans for revising papers. Instead of seeing this uncertainty as a kind of scholarly positioning where claiming a lack of knowledge keeps options open, where tentativeness leads to questioning and developing knowledge, I saw it as defeat, frustration, avoidance, and resistance. When I had time to reflect, to think hard about the context for each declaration of "I don't know," I remembered an incident in a class with Dr. B. I had finally offered a response to a question, and Dr. B., perhaps sensing some latent insight in my answer, began with a series of questions to attempt to lead me to new knowledge. Frustrated after struggling to answer only a few of these, frightened by the attention of the teacher and my classmates, feeling put on the spot, I finally blurted out: "Beats the hell outta me!", a response simultaneously submissive—a retreat from questioning—and yet aggressive in its use of profanity. Trapped, I was angry and scared. I remember how my classmates turned away from me in shock, and Dr. B., momentarily silent , narrowed one eye and tilted his head in a look that I read as disgust. He turned away, and I have no memory of being called on or speaking aloud again in that class. Even now, understanding more about teaching and learning, power, gender, and class relations, I can feel the humiliation of the moment and the relief of silence, can feel the sense of disgrace that I believed I carried about me like a shroud of failure for the rest of the semester.

With nowhere to go in a conference, my female students retreated as I had into "I don't know." I don't have videotapes of these conferences, so I can't say what my face registered. My voice registered frustration, for unlike Dr. B., I didn't have a class to turn to. The women disavowed knowledge, ability, and direction more than once—they had to, for I had only them to badger and they had no class to hide in.

My male students used a different linguistic approach, heading me off at the pass, so to speak. After telling me what they were planning to do with their drafts, they indicated no uncertainty, only enthusiasm. I mistook their confidence for ability and knowledge, and didn't even think, as I was speaking with them, about the benefits they might experience from questioning their decisions. They had answers to my questions; whether they were well thought out or not, I didn't take the time to find out. It was enough that they had answered, for then I could continue on in a teacherly march to cover their papers (I certainly wasn't *dis-covering* anything new about them, for I didn't allow students to pursue in any depth any topic that concerned them). I sensed during the conferences that there was a momentum with male students, a feeling of progress that didn't occur with female students. Here is that linear movement again, the need to press forward coupled with an almost unconscious gratitude and positive response for students who help that happen.

In my colleagues' conferences, questions about gender arise in many ways. The counts of features that served as a jumping off point for more reflection indicate, for example, that while certainly teachers control talk in conferences, gender alters that control in interesting ways. Taken together, these features create a remarkably complex picture.

Gender and Conferencing: Female Students

In almost every case, discourse markers are used much more frequently with female students than male students. Although a higher
frequency of use with female students is to be expected, given that
there are two more female students in this study than male students,
the differences are striking: *and* is used twice as frequently with
female students, *you know* occurs five times as frequently, and *well*
almost three times as frequently. Female students were more tentative about their knowledge when speaking with male teachers, using
the phrase "I don't know" 22 times with males, but only twice with
the same number of female teachers. They were slightly more likely
to ask a male teacher what he thought than they were to ask a female
teacher. Furthermore, female students overlapped cooperatively
with male instructors almost four times more frequently than with
female instructors. In doing so, they indicate not only the strict
attention they are paying to the male partners but their willingness
to assist the male teacher in continuing to speak. In all these
instances, female students perform "feminine" gender with male
teachers in ways that correspond to traditional sociolinguistic folklore, such as "women speak more than men do": their cooperative
overlaps register consciously with male teachers as support and
encouragement. Talk by women students averaged 24.4% of all talk
in conferences with male teachers, but only 13.6% of conferences
with female teachers. Asking more qustions, denying their own
knowledge, and asking for the male teacher's opinion and knowledge all helped to position the teacher as an active male expert and
the student as a passive female learner.

If female students are speaking in stereotypical ways to their male
teachers, it would seem difficult for these teachers to respond in any
less traditional ways. In order to be appropriately responsive, the listener is predicting and constructing the speaker, drawing on previous experience both with this particular speaker and with the
community the speaker represents. It is not surprising, then, that
male teachers are more likely than female teachers to interrupt
female students. Male teachers are more likely to use the discourse
markers *well* and *but* with their female students than with male students, both frequent indicators of disagreement when applied to
another's speech and of complication and repair when a speaker
uses them to respond to his or her own speech. Male teachers are

also much more likely to use the relationship markers *you know* and *I mean* with their female students than with their male students. While *you know* can assume shared knowledge and thus be a form of praise, it can also be—as we've seen—a way to force students into a cognitive relationship they find difficult to resist. The use of *I mean* can mark not just the attempt to clarify speech, but a preoccupation with the speaker. *I mean* also functions as a place holder, keeping other parties from self-selecting, from joining in the talk. Thus, depending upon the interpretation, *I mean* indicates either a concern for the listener (explaining a belief that she doesn't understand) or a lack of interest in the listener.

My first, gut-level reaction to this data was to see it as double domination, teacher/student, male/female: male teachers dominating female students, controlling their speech, disagreeing with them, forcing them into a shared position and simultaneously reinforcing a hierarchy based on their educational capital. My second response was to ask why female students would participate in such a situation (if such a situation did exist) unless they felt they gained something from it. But as I thought about my own experiences as an undergraduate, I realized that I didn't see myself as an active participant in such social and power relations. Rather, I saw the traditional relation of teacher and student as "right" and "natural." Positioning myself within those structures, I willingly participated in my own domination, only occasionally and vaguely aware I was doing so.

Perhaps, too, female students didn't feel disempowered and dominated, but performed a role that would get them what they needed in order to be successful in their writing classes. That is, they felt that if they could not control the classroom or the university, they could at least control the conference. Fully aware of the response they would elicit by performing in stereotypically feminine ways, they gambled that the rewards would be greater than the punishment, that their cooperative and supportive behavior would prompt the teacher to provide more information about the "right" interpretation of the text under discussion, as well as more guidelines and conventions to ensure that their next revision or paper would meet with approval. If that sounds manipulative or conniving, even unbelievable, I only have to think about the number of times students have told me how they get the teacher off track in class by asking the right kind of question at the right time. I only have to think about graduate school and calculating, like my peers, how I would handle

an upcoming conference with a demanding or intimidating professor. I got advice from people who had experience—"Here's what you
do...." So I won't completely discount any of these possible responses
and interpretations of the data. I think they are all both problematic
and occasionally valid.

Consider in the example below how Dana's tentativeness elicits
help from Eric, and how he interrupts her to provide that help. In
this excerpt, Dana has been telling Eric that she is concerned because
when she writes, she uses exclusively an organizational structure she
learned in high school.

539 Dana: An I (tapping paper) THIS is an example of it, I mean, cause
540   like I took a I took e- um, a paragraph for each woman, and
541 Eric: ⌊Mm-hmm
542 Dana: that's the kind of structure we stuck to in uh in high school, but
543   then I guess I guess there's a difference though in the type of
544   paper I'm talking about, because last semester the papers were
545   more um, like personal stories, that kind of ⌈thing, and so I don't
546 Eric: ⌊Yeah
547 Dana: know, there were things that come up like in in conferences
548   with, I had a grad student ⌈last semester, and um, she was like
549 Eric: ⌊Yeah?
550 Dana: you know, this is very, uh what's mechanical or something and
551   and but I knew that if I'd taken it to maybe like, a⌈freshman high
552 Eric: ⌊Yeah
553 Dana: school teacher ⌈she would have liked it⌈And, I mean obviously
554 Eric: ⌊Yeah   ⌊Yeah
555 Dana: there's a there's a difference in you know, maturity in writing
556   but--
557 Eric: ⌊Well, uh okay, I mean, it should sound like the, the paper
558   should sound like i- it comes from a person, I mean, your paper
559   shouldn't sound like Heidi's or Ben's papers, or ⌈somebody else,
560 Dana: ⌊Mm-hmm
561 Eric: I mean I should know who's writing the paper there should be a
562   a person in the paper, and so one meaning of "this is very
563   mechanical" uh, could mean that the, that you know the
564   language is so abstract, that there's so many impersonal verbs,
565   there's so many passive voices, I don't know what that, I uh it's
566   hard to think of a person as having written this rather than my
567   insurance com⌈pany talling me how much ⌈money I have in my
568 Dana: ⌊Right   ⌊Mmm
569 Eric: account by way of a computer. Okay.

Eric goes on to explain that in a literature class, students need to create an argument, and suggests ways of laying out that argument.

Dana uses a double *I guess* in line 543 and *I don't know* in line 545, searches for a word in line 550, and hedges on her descriptions of a different reading community in lines 551 and 556. She indicates that her teacher last semester was a graduate student, perhaps a way of indicating the teacher's knowledge was questionable next to Eric's, a full professor with 25 years of experience. In fact, Eric responds with interest to that information, with a full questioning intonation to his "Yeah?" Dana's use of *but* in line 556 indicates that she is going on to problematize her "obviously" in line 555, just as she used *but* in line 542, second guessing her statement of knowledge. All these are ways of indicating uncertainty, and Eric responds not just with a discussion of voice and passivity in writing, but with a lesson on framing an argument—all valuable information for a first-year student struggling with her writing. How much of this dynamic structure Eric and Dana are aware of I can't tell. But just as we learn that we need to speak in particular ways to parents or peers to get certain responses and results, in our many years of schooling we learn patterns of speech that are "appropriate" to gendered academic interactions and are designed to elicit the responses we want.

Consider the ways in which Cari's overlaps with Bill in the transcript excerpt we looked at in chapter two urge him to continue to speak; she is so interested in what he is saying that she is attempting to predict it, to move it ahead. Cooperative overlaps indicate shared knowledge (if not agreement), and Cari may be trying to indicate her understanding of Bill's reasoning, though she is not always successful in doing so. In her conference with Don, Eva's initial question about her paper goes unanswered for almost the entire conference as Don considers aspects of the novel that interest him. Eva does not interrupt him; she insistently yet carefully asks questions about the material, indicating an interest in what he is saying yet turning the conversation slowly back to her original question. In fact, as the tape runs out, she is asking another question. Questioning can be very powerful, particularly if you ignore an answer and repeat a question, thus dismissing the answer. But it can also function more subtly. We ask questions when we are interested in a story. When the questions consistently connect to the material, we are encouraging the speaker to continue. So Don talks at length with Eva as she moves the talk in a large circle back to what she needs to know. With Don, Lyn suddenly shifts, the tone of the conference to conversation, catching Don off guard as she makes a statement with the tone of a question that she likes the book they had discussed. Don responds with "Huh?" but goes on to develop the topic, and Lyn supports him, as she has throughout the conference.

My sense of these conferences between male teachers and female students mirrors in one aspect my sense of all conferences—that control and performances shift from moment to moment in an intricate dance between participants. But these are congenial, full of advice, and the control of the teacher is not challenged; rather, it is supported.

But then a question arises concerning the ways in which female students interact with female teachers. Do female students not perform in stereotypically female ways with female teachers because there's no reward in doing so? Because there's no punishment for not performing in a way that a female teacher will recognize as a performance—in other words, they don't need to "perform" in order to avoid punishment? Feminist theorists have often claimed that speech between women is cooperative, supportive, non-competeitive, nurturing, and recursive. This claim has been made across a variety of contexts: women's studies seminars, women's gossip sessions, meetings between women administrators or managers. But these characterizations often rest on a fundamental gender binary that has been called into question and on the cultural descriptions of women that result from this binary: if male speech is often full of conflict and challenge, female speech will be the opposite; if women are non-competitive, then their speech will be non-competitive.

These conferences and my own experiences in conferencing do not provide such a simple picture. In terms of word count alone, female teachers dominate female students just as male teachers do. Female teachers are less likely to interrupt their female students than male teachers are, but they are also less likely to cooperatively overlap their speech. Female students initiate fewer revision strategies to female teachers and hear less praise from female teachers. Finally, they hear and use less discipline-specific terminology with female teachers than male teachers. All this together does not add up to the picture of cooperation, support, and shared control that is often presented as characteristic of female-to-female speech. However, the data may also indicate that in this setting, female students don't feel they have to work as hard in conferences with female teachers. They may feel they don't have to introduce as many topics, they don't have to be so cooperative, they don't have to prove they are serious about their writing by offering as many strategies for revison or using the terminology that demonstrates their "fitness" for the community represented by the teacher. In one important aspect—their gender— they are already a part of the community represented by the teacher.

But because conferencing so closely resembles teaching, not con- versation, the roles of teacher and student seem to dominate, while gender roles complicate. In Erin and Leah's conference, for example, Erin's role as teacher and her desire to see Leah's paper move in a par- ticular direction is foregrounded, not the connections perhaps possi- ble because both participants are female.

314	Erin:	(Continuing turn) And you're right he
315		he does use the fact that Marx is becoming more more vulnerable.
316		(2 sec) You might wanna work in here too why Marx is more
317		vulnerable. You know, why:.. Is he taking stock of his religion.
318		in a way that he seemingly hasn't. At least I get the impression
319		that it's been a a number of years since he's even thought about
320		it.
321	Leah:	⌈Alright./
322	Erin:	⌊And ki- kind of in an ironically it's Grossbart who who makes
323		him--
324	Leah:	Right, right
325	Erin:	So in a kind of twisted way he is defender of the faith, wouldn't
326		you say?
327	Leah:	(2 sec) Yeah I guess.
328	Erin:	So because of so because his his um behavior
329	Leah:	/Nye:ah guess/
330	Erin:	prompts Marx to re-evaluate his own stance about his religion.
331		That's something you can explore. Kay.

Leah's "Alright" in line 321 is very soft, tentative. She interrupts Erin, indicating that she knows where Erin is heading with this. On the tape, her voice is exasperated. After Erin offers her interpretation of who the real "defender of the faith" is, she adds a tag that attempts to force agreement—"wouldn't you say?" But Leah continues to resist, while Erin presses her point using *so* with conclusive force, as if agreement has been met. Leah's original interpretation has been dis- carded by the teacher, and her response to the enforced agreement is essentially to withdraw from the conference. For the next 110 lines of speech—almost to the end of the conference—her responses are minimal unless asked a direct question.

Gender and Conferencing: Male Students

Male students challenged the control of female instructors in many ways. The proportion of student to teacher speech was slightly higher between male students and female teachers than male students and male teachers: 23.4% and 20.1% respectively. Further, with the exception of the markers *Oh* and *I mean*, male students were much more likely to use discourse markers to control conference talk with female teachers than with male teachers. Male students use *and* more forcefully to hold the floor, mark an upcoming utterance as possible disagreement with *well*, and are more insistent on their own perspective. Male students were much more likely to interrupt their female teachers than their male teachers. Female teacher-male student dyads were much more likely to produce cooperative overlaps than male-male dyads. However, many of these completions on the part of male students seemed designed to demonstrate their knowledge to the female teacher. In keeping with this use of the cooperative overlap, male students were less tentative of their knowledge in conferences with female teacher, less likely to say "I don't know" with them than their male teachers.

The female teachers' responses to these challenges to their power are mixed and very complex. On the one hand, the cooperative overlaps and the seeming lack of response to male students' use of controlling discourse markers (female teachers were no more likely to interrupt and gain or regain the floor with male students than male teachers were) appears to indicate that female teachers accept a more equal relationship with male students than they do with female students. And, interestingly, female teachers were more likely than male teachers to say "I don't know" when conferencing with male students. On the other hand, while the number of revision strategies and rules and conventions female teachers offer to male students is comparable to what they offer to female students, the lack of praise (less than offered to female students) may indicate a general displeasure with their male students' performance in writing—and perhaps with their performance in conferencing? It may also be a response to the stance of certainty adopted by so many male students; they don't need praise to build their confidence.

The response of female teachers seems to be a balancing act between the control that teachers conventionally exert over students and the deference and support that women are supposed to show men. Thus there is often a sense of struggle in the conferences between female teachers and male students that isn't present in conferences between these same female teachers and their female students. The control that female teachers exert over female students is never in question though it may not be welcomed, as we heard in Erin and Leah's conference. The control they maintain over male students, however, is often subtly challenged. In the excerpt below from Nina and John's conference, John both supports and challenges Nina.

188 John: Does it matter how much longer the papers get?
189 Nina: No. There there's no ma maximum length you know.
190 John: ⌊Oh, okay. Because   ⌊That's-
191   some classes like especially in high school well they said three
192   pages and they docked you if it's four
193 Nina: ⌊No
194 John: ⌊or three and a half.
195 Nina: ⌊No.
196 John: That's pretty much why well it cause it was kind of a condition. I
197   like to write like this. I like to (2 sec) I like to write scientific
198 Nina: ⌊Mm-hmm
199 John: and.. You know political science papers where I can just (makes a
200   noise like fast scribbling) this is what happened. This
201   caused this. And so it's really been kind of tough for me in
202 Nina: Right, right.
203 John: ⌊English to go on all my thought processes and drag things up
204 Nina: ⌊Mm-hmm
205 John: cause (voice trails off).
206 Nina: Right. Right. Well, I think it's just that it that question also it's
207   like you know cause you've gotta keep in mind that that the
208   person reading this paper doesn't have access to your mind or
209   access to your comments, to talk to talk you so you when you say
210 John: ⌊I know that
211 Nina: I don't like dogs it might be a good idea to give the reason why
212 John: ⌊Explain
213 Nina: you don't like dogs right. I doesn't have to be incredibly
214 John: ⌊/why/ Sure.
215 Nina: personal- (tape stops, then resumes). Okay, um so do you have
216   any questions then?

217 John: (2 sec) No. I know I have to go all over all my papers and.. read
218   it as someone esle. Uh distance myself.
219 Nina: It's also a good idea to have you and your roommate through and
220   have him mark by anything he doesn't isn't quite sure of you
221   know.]
222 John: ⌐Yeah it's I've had kind of difficulties with peer.. peer..
223   uh doing papers with your friends and stuff cause they a lot of
224   times they'll just say oh yeah it's a good paper--
225 Nina: I like it. I know.
226 John: And.. And it.. You know cause it's kind of hard to rip someone
227   apart.
229 Nina: Well I don't I don't know why people think of this in the sense
230   of ripping them apart when you say to them I d- just say to them
231   I don't understand this point. It's not like a personal attack like
232   you dirty dog you know ⌐
233 John: └Well different people have
234 difficulties / ? /--
235 Nina: └I know. Oh I know they're very people can be very sensitive
236   about their writing. Um.. Gee (2 sec) Well um so everything I
237   said to you you you it made sense to you right?
238 John: It makes sense to me now and hopefully it'll
239 Nina: ┌Right.
240 John: └I'll retain everything when I go uh make all my revisions.⌐
241 Nina: └Do
242   you listen to the tapes again?
243 John: That helps a lot.
244 Nina: Okay.⌐
245 John: └A lot.⌐
246 Nina: └So
247 John: It's but still you know.. I do that and I do
248   everything on the tape and.. It still like doesn't turn out exactly
249 Nina: └It
250 John: ┌what I want/
251 Nina: └takes time you know.
252 John: └Oh I know I know
253 Nina: So.
254 John: But the tapes do help.
255 Nina: Yeah well then good good. Okay then I will (2 sec) It's the END
256   Laurel.
Conference Ends

John begins this segment by asking about page length, then interrupts Nina to explain why he asked the question, perhaps concerned

that she will interpret his question as a complaint about having to write long papers. He continues to explain even as Nina tells him "no" twice. At this point, they are speaking simultaneously. Without any coordinating or contrasting marker, John abruptly switches the topic to the kind of writing he likes: scientific essays with the kinds of cause and result statements that he apparently finds easier to produce than the personal narratives with analysis that he's done in English (he doesn't say "in your class" to Nina, but it's understood). He refers to the process of supporting statements, which Nina has asked him to work on earlier in the conference, as "dragging things up." Although Nina acknowledges his feelings, she hints at displeasure or disagreement with his assessment and attempts to explain the needs of an audience (she has been the audience so far). John interrupts her in line 210 to assert that he already knows that, but Nina ignores his interruption and continues. This time, John offers proof that he *does* know what she means, by producing a cooperative overlap.

When Nina suggests a revising strategy in line 219, John at first appears to agree with or support her ("yeah") but actually goes on to disagree. This time Nina produces the cooperative overlap, but John continues, holding his place with *and*. When he suggests that giving peer advice consists of "ripping someone apart," Nina immediately disagrees with him. John defends his position, latching his own *well* onto Nina's *you know*, thus asserting that he does not share the perspective she has offered him. Nina asserts that she understands his position, but moves the argument to a more distant ground, to "people" generally as opposed to John and his classmates.

Near the end of the conference, John indicates his concern about his ability to revise. As I've noted, uncertainty when used by a student appears to be a successful way to provoke a helpful response, and Nina suggests he listen to the tapes she makes in place of written comments. He praises the tapes repeatedly, but complains that though he listens to them and does exactly what she suggests, he still doesn't produce the kind of paper he wants—or she wants; the conference tape isn't clear. This is a challenge to Nina's ability to critique, not a suggestion that John may not write well. Nina's response is to interrupt him and assert obliquely that John has unrealistic expectations. John, in turn, overlaps his speech, asserting that he *does* know that writing well takes time. He then goes on to restate how helpful the tapes are. Nina's response suggests she has to work herself up to support John's final assertion, as it is no longer believable. The challenges to Nina's power as teacher are subtle but frequent.

In two of the three conferences between male teachers and male students, it seems as if the gender of the instructor may have combined with the power of his position to limit performance options available to the students. In many contexts, cultural constructs for males involve asserting dominance. In conferences with female instructors, the gender of the instructor undermines at least slightly the power of her position as teacher, thus permitting male students to perform in some dominant ways. When the power of the teacher is supported by gender, however, then performing dominance becomes more difficult for male students. Performing submission— or supporting dominance—while an option for many women, is not generally a part of the male repertoire. This perhaps explains why Ben and Dave accept Eric and Carl's criticsm and praise, neither challenging them nor playing an active role in shaping the form of their interpretations and evaluations. They cannot easily challenge a male teacher, but they cannot submit, either, and so their participation is limited. And because the teacher shapes the conference as teaching, not conversation, the students cannot imagine any other possible roles for themselves.

Mike, on the other hand, offers resistance at various points throughout the entire conference, responding incompletely or not at all to conference opening questions, disagreeing with Bill's criticism, and challenging the course grade even as Bill is constructing it. The two often talk over each other, interrupting and insisting on speaking rights. This conference stands out from the other thirteen for the extent of its opposition, both active and passive. In fact, as the conference closes, Bill tells Mike that at this point he's got a "B" in the course. Mike responds: "And I- well, okay, I don't see it going much further than that. Awright, that's cool." He refuses to participate in traditional ways, instead taking control of his grade by deciding how much work he is willing and able to do with this teacher, determining for himself the value of his time and writing.

What's the Outcome?

Significant issues arise from all this talk about gender: Students as well as texts are evaluated in conferences; assessment takes many forms, some of which are overt but most of which are much more subtle; and assessment patterns and learning patterns appear to be connected to gender.

Until recently, I naively thought I was really only counting *attendance* at a conference as part of my students' course participation, and that "assessment" meant, finally and most importantly for the student, grades. And I continued to think so, even after conducting discourse analysis on my own conferences. It wasn't until I began to study conferences between other teachers and their students that I realized, as I read through pages of transcripts, in how many ways I was evaluating these students. And if I was doing so, so must their instructors, who will actually give them a grade, who will approach their writing and speech with a new assessment of the student after each conference.

It's easier—at least for me—to see more clearly what goes on in conference assessment if I think about the ways in which I've been assessed. For example, if I'm talking with a colleague about a teaching practice I've come up with, and the colleague nods and says, "Great idea!" that's clearly positive evaluation. But there are other ways of assessing.

One of the things I remember about Thanksgiving when I was young is that the little kids sat at the folding card table in the kitchen, and the adults got the big table in the dining room. I remember very clearly the first Thanksgiving when I was not only allowed to sit at the big table while we ate, but no one asked me to leave when the plates were taken away and the talk began. I sat there saying nothing but listening to the adults. No one "watched" their language, and while I may not have been an active participant, I was brought into a circle of adult speech and exposed to terms, concepts, and ways of interacting that acknowledged me as at least a marginal member of that group. That, too, was assessment; not as obvious as explicit praise, but a positive judgement that I was mature enough to be admitted to that community of adults.

We are all familiar with qualified praise: "You did this well enough, but..." In fact, as I've listened surreptitiously to students in peer groups, I've heard them mimicking me, mimicking other teachers, saying that same phrase with wide-eyed sarcasm and snickering with one another. Most of us would recognize, in our annual evaluation, that receiving a lot of such praise meant we weren't being praised at all. There are other kinds of negative evaluation. For example, while I was interviewing for a position years ago, one of the interviewers asked me several times as I spoke if I could "back up a bit" and clarify something I'd said. While such a request indicates interest, it's also a negative assessment of my ability to gauge my audience's needs, to organize my material in ways that make sense to others.

How do these kinds of assessments manifest themselves in a conference? One way is by the instructor's use of discipline-specific terminology, the words that have special meaning in a composition or literary context. For example, to support a claim in English is very different from supporting a beam in carpentry. Words such as "freewrite," "revise," "peer group," "develop," "substance," and even "interrogate" would be discipline-specific terms. Using these terms without any explanation indicates—like the Thanksgiving scene—that the speaker assumes the listener is a part of her community. Using and defining them indicates a willingness to help the listener become part of the speaker's community; not using them at all in a setting where we would expect them indicates that the speaker does not consider the listener to be a member of her community. Likewise, requests for clarification and extensive suggestions for revision or correction indicate an assessment that the writer has not organized or presented information in ways that are "conventional" or expected by the instructor.

All of this is really nothing new; I am aware that I am assessing when I write marginal comments, and I go back through to see if I have balanced my praise and criticism if possible. But in the real-time of conferencing, we rarely reflect on the structure of our speech or the "amount" of any particular kind of speech. We tend to function more unconsciously, aware of subtle shifts. For example, a student may begin to respond in single words as she resists a revision suggestion. We may eventually become aware of this pattern and respond, perhaps not changing our position but finding more to praise in the student's paper, perhaps allowing the student to speak and explain her own position.

Assessment and praise appear to be complexly linked to gender in these conferences. Female students are praised much more frequently than male students, particularly in terms of unqualified praise. Additionally, female students receive many more suggestions for revision than do male students, in both higher order and lower order categories, and propose or test more revision strategies than do their male peers. They are much more likely to hear discipline-specific language and use it in return in their conferences. Finally, female students are more likely to be supplied with the rules, definitions, and conventions that help writers establish themselves in the discourse of a discipline.

It's possible to make connections here, to see some patterns developing. As female students suggest revision strategies to their instructors, instructors first respond typically by evaluating the strategy (usually involving some praise of one kind or another), and then by offering a counter-strategy, additional strategies, or variations on the student strategy. As instructors conclude their response, there is another evaluation (although sometimes the object of praise here is mixed, as they are praising their own strategies as well as the student's!). Because female students are more likely than males to put forth their revision strategies in the form of questions or in an uncertain tone or to devalue those strategies, instructors are more likely to respond at length, not merely to evaluate. They offer help in addition to evaluation. As instructors outline strategies, they use the terminology of the discipline, and as their responses lengthen, they move from text-specific commentary to the rules and conventions of the discipline. They may also move into new knowledge for themselves, working through an idea that has suddenly occurred to them; speaking largely to themselves, they use the language familiar to them. As female students repeat back these strategies and ideas or suggest new ones, they use the terminology they have just heard applied to their own papers and writing processes. And they leave the conference with a set of guidelines—that a good place to start a paper is with your own reactions to the text, assertions can be made with the proper evidence, one of the tests for meaning is redundancy—to help them rewrite this paper and move to the next one.

Male students, on the other hand, speak in ways that do not elicit the same kinds of language from the instructors as the female students. Male students ask fewer questions to clarify a previous statement made by an instructor, offer fewer revision strategies as questions and few revision strategies overall. Mike, Jeff, and John, for example, all defend the strategies they used in writing their papers. Instead of the cooperative development of instructor-suggested revision strategies that occurs more frequently in conferences with female students, the male students tended either to resist the suggestions offered by their teachers or to agree without extensive elaboration. So, in this small group of students and teachers, it appears that female students are entering conferences with interaction strategies that allow them to leave those conferences with revising ideas and language that will help them succeed in their composition classes.

Gender Inequity

Acknowledging the traditional power relations between teachers and students and males and females, female students in these conferences receive the kind of guidance that both firmly embeds them in the conventional social structure and rewards them for accepting that position—even as it disadvantages them. Both teachers and students draw on their experiences in gendered classrooms as they meet to talk in conferences.

Gender inequity in the classroom is well documented, even to the point of appearing in popular literature. Not long ago, when an all-female college went coed, the newspapers carried accounts of the changes in classroom interaction occasioned by the entrance of men. Sadker and Sadker (1984, 1986) have extensively documented gender bias in the classroom. In a study of more than one hundred fourth-, sixth-, and eighth-grade classrooms—a sample that included urban, suburban, and rural schools, classes both homogeneous and racially/ethnically varied, and courses in languages arts, social studies, and math—they observed the "pervasiveness" of sex bias. Male students were involved in more interactions with their teachers, received more attention, and received more precise feedback on their responses to teachers—more remediation, more praise, more criticism.

But why this is so is not always clear, and it will surely take a great deal more study to figure out. In one study of an elementary classroom (Swann, 1988), the teacher adhered to a rule that she would call on whoever got their hand up first, thus supposedly allowing males and females an equal chance. However, after viewing videotapes of the class interaction, Swann noted that subtle clues from the teacher, such as eye contact, eyebrow raising, and body posture, cued male students first that a question was forthcoming. Consistently and unconsciously alerted, male students raised their hands before the female students. Thus, male students had more opportunities to interact with the teacher, to receive feedback, and to test their knowledge.

Follow-up studies on gender, teaching, and learning at the college level, both broadly based and narrowly focused, indicate that the pattern of sex bias persists. These studies indicate such bias is both conscious and unconscious. Most women I've spoken to have some horror story to tell about sexism in the classroom; I have my own. And if the students I spoke with years ago when I first began studying my own conferencing had been more aware of language patterns, they might have been able to articulate their frustration with the gendered interaction of our conferences.

Sexism is about power, and power and gender appear to be (at the moment) inextricably intertwined. Many early claims about "women's language" have been reconsidered. O'Barr and Atkins (1983), for example, examined language use in the courtroom and found that the speech of defendants often manifested the same kinds of features that Robin Lakoff (1975) ascribed to "women's language." A number of research studies have indicated that "power differences masquerade as gender differences because women in this society usually possess limited power or status compared with men (Simkins-Bullock and Wildman, 1991).

While a great deal of research on classroom interaction has focused on gender relations, such issues are largely unacknowledged in conferencing studies. For example, in Freedman and Sperling's study of high- and low-achieving students, it seems important to me to ask why the high-achieving male, Jay, receives expository modeling in an academic register, while the high-achieving female, Sherry, receives expository modeling in a colloquial register. Hearing such modeling in an academic register, Jay is exposed to the use of high-value words—discipline-specific terminology—as well as the articulation of conventions of writing. Sherry, on the other hand, hears the conventions but does not hear the language that carries weight in a community that evaluates her not only on her use of those conventions but on her ability to discuss them. Jay receives an invitation to return to discuss his ideas or to ask for clarification on concepts the teacher may not have explained clearly. Sherry also receives an invitation to return, *first*, however, if *she* doesn't understand a concept or is confused (there is no indication that the teacher might have played a role in the confusion), and *then* if she has an idea to discuss. Unlike Jay, Sherry receives two warnings that she must keep up with the class work, although she is a high-achieving student. It seems important, too, that Jay's self-generalizations are positive, while the females in this study, regardless of level of achievement, make negative self-generalization. The possible relations of gender and achievement and gendered response (both teacher and student) go unremarked.

We have so little information on conferencing and gender that it's hard to say why the male students in my research didn't receive the kind of discipline-specific language and academic modeling that the male student in Freedman and Sperling's study did. Perhaps the "get to know you" atmosphere of the first conference of the semester, which they chose to study, prompted more speech from the males and maybe a bit more tentativeness? Perhaps the teacher responded to her high-achieving male student as I did, considering him a "Writer" and making the same mistake I did—not recognizing the expertise of the high-achieving female.

Wong (1989), too, explores a relationship between tutor and tutee where power appears to be solely a function of participants' academic roles, where gender and other important social constructs apparently do not enter the talk. While I can identify the gender of the tutors, I am not positive of the gender of the student in two of the four conferences she examine. Nonetheless, it seems worthwhile to pursue the issue of gender, for the two conferences in which the knowledge of the tutee is recognized and respected involve the female tutor, while the two in which the tutee's knowledge base is ignored or co-opted involve the male tutor.

Again, in Walker and Elias's study of high- and low-rated conferences, gender is surprisingly a non-issue. In the lowest rated conferences, all but one is between a male tutor and a female tutee, and in the highly rated conferences, there is only one with a mixed gender. In a re-analysis of the transcripts, Gail Stygall (1998) argues that both high- and low-rated conferences are affected by gender roles and expectations. In examining topic control in both kinds of conferences, she finds that the male tutor remains in control throughout, repeatedly ignoring attempts at a topic switch by the female student in an exchange common to male-female talk across speech situations. Further, the male tutors both ask double or even triple questions, which Stygall notes is common in doctor-patient exchanges where there is a similar asymmetry of power. In the highly rated conference, the teacher dominates the amount of talk: 62% to the student's 38%. This figure closely matches the ratio of talk between males and females that Spender (1989) argues is comfortable for both sexes. Such a re-analysis, from a critically informed position, problematizes a relationship previously constructed on academic roles only. As

Stygall points out, socialization takes place both inside the classroom (and conference) and outside, and that includes socialization in gender roles as well as institutional roles.

Some conference studies point to simple turn-taking and the apparent opportunity for both student and teacher to initiate topics as indicative of conversational dialogue and horizontal power relations. But as we saw in chapter one, to assume that a conference is a conversation on the basis of turn-taking alone is simplistic, for conversation involves more than that, and most speech interaction involves taking turns of one kind or another. And to assume that students have the same opportunities to initiate topics as their teachers flies in the face of the very transcripts that are presented as evidence. In excerpt after excerpt, the teacher controls the topic and access to the floor. The same is true of conversation between males and females. Contrary to the folklore, numerous studies indicate that when men and women talk, men talk more than women. Women introduce more topics than men but rarely are they taken up for discussion (an aspect of the affective dimension of conferencing we'll take up in chapter five); furthermore, women have to do most or all of the necessary tasks to keep a conversation going—what Pamela Fishman (1977) calls "interactional shitwork."

In the conferences I recorded, institutional roles are foregrounded over gender roles; gender does not, however, go unacknowledged or unperformed. Rather, patterns of control and gender are closely and complexly intertwined, and examining these patterns and the results sheds some light why conferences may not be as successful as we hope. One issue to consider is "gender performance."

Judith Butler (1992) problematizes the traditional binary concept of gender by asserting that gender is performative. Most debates about gender parallel "nature versus nurture" arguments, considering gender as either a biological or a cultural construct. The line between the two becomes blurred, however, when we consider that no human is ever "out of" a culture. Ultimately, what is left out of this debate and the picture of gender that emerges is agency and the role of shifting contexts. Butler plays with the terms of this debate, asserting that we "perform" a "feminine" or "masculine" gender to meet external expectation or satisfy our "psychological gender." She points out that in many ways we "cross-dress" and perform another gender, but unless we are performing the psychological gender we feel, the cross-dressing is *not* the performance—the "conventional" dress is the performance. She posits the possibility of multiple genders, growing out of the postmodern concept of multiple selves and multiple contexts. Our performance is tied to the context, to the reward for performing in a certain way, and to the punishment for performing in unexpected, unconventional, or undesirable ways.

Of course, there are conflicting expectations and rewards. For example, when a boy "calls out" in an elementary classroom, he is often rewarded by being allowed to speak, to address the topic on the floor or answer a question without being selected by the teacher, even if he is also given a reprimand. When a girl calls out, she is more likely to be reprimanded and refused access to the floor—a double punishment. However, if she raises her hand, she risks not being called upon at all. Thus, while she avoids punishment by not calling out, she may also receive no reward for behaving in the expected manner—unless we consider the absence of punishment a reward in itself. To do so, however, seems clearly psychologically and pedagogically unhealthy. Likewise, I have had female students tell me that they are reluctant to challenge male classmates, to demand a speaking turn free of interruptions, to insist that the topics they offer be considered as seriously as those offered by males, and to request that their male peers share equally the work of critiquing a classmate's paper in a peer group. They understand the rewards of such behavior, but they fear the consequences—they they will be labeled a "bitch" by both male and female classmates. And so they perform "feminine" gender for the class, hoping that their classmates won't see it as a performance (which would have a negative result) and that I *will* (which hopefully will have a positive result, given what they perceive I value). Women are well aware of the linguistic and cultural domination of males and can "play the game," perform as expected—but at what price? Sociological and linguistic research shows that males, too, must perform, but performing from a culturally dominant position generally provides them with more options.

There are problems with Butler's argument. For example, the use of the word "perform" implies a consciousness of gender constructs, a premeditation that I don't believe is always present. Additionally, her focus on gender and performance doesn't adequately consider the interaction of gender constructs with institutional or other social constructs. For example, I don't always see myself as a woman teaching; sometimes I see myself simply as a teacher. My unawareness of my gender doesn't mean that others are not aware of it, nor does it mean that it isn't affecting my teaching, but I am not consciously choosing to perform as a female teacher. Nonetheless, one of the values of Butler's argument is that it complicates a debate that has often been reductive and essentialistic. It forces me to consider students and teachers as active constructors of these conferences, as persons both aware of some of the linguistic options open to them as as male and female speakers and yet still deeply embedded in the constructs that shape our culture and these conferences.

Acknowledging Gender, Improving Conferences

Perhaps critical reflection on gender, power, and discourse is most difficult to achieve in conferencing. After all, we have been performing gender and culture all our lives in many ways, for many more years than we have been in the institutional roles of students or teachers. We are so accustomed to these roles that we can rarely see or feel them. In fact, despite the differences by gender here— female students receiving more praise, more suggestions for revision, more rules than males—both genders felt the conferences were successful. Perhaps what counts as successful is different for males than females; I don't think I have enough information to answer that. While cultural expectations for males and females might lead me to say that women are expected to be supportive and cooperative while males are expected to be dominant, aggressive, and controlling, that's certainly not how females and males consistently behaved in these conferences. Rather, their behaviors were constantly shifting. Is there then some set of gendered guidelines with which we all work, some boundary beyond which behavior is "marked" as unacceptable or which causes discomfort? Do we construct the behavior of our partners to fit these guidelines until they cross that boundary, thus reading women's requests for clarification, for example, not as possible disagreement or aggression or criticism but as cooperation and support? I have to admit that I initially read the agreement that Jeff offers Erin as "too much," and nicknamed him "the weasel" (only briefly, until I did some more thinking). I seriously have to consider that if it had been a female student offering agreement to Erin, I might not even have marked it, might have considered it "ordinary," supportive behavior from a woman. It's easy for me in this book to call for critical reflection on gender during the conference, but when I find it so difficult to do so with tapes, transcripts, and the time to reflect, how difficult a task I and other teachers will find it to be in our own practice!

But address it we must. Teachers who explicitly discuss gender in their classrooms know that students will quickly offer them the folk-lore about gender and language: women's chattiness, male silence, gendered topics, women interested in talking about feelings and males avoiding it, etc. But articulating folklore alone will not generate change or awareness of the ways in which gender positively or negatively affects the shape or outcome of speech events. Most students reject research that challenges folklore or that asks them to rethink in important ways the structure that supports their self-constructions. So simply presenting research on male-female interruptions or topic development isn't enough.

It's important for students to test new claims, to experience research. They can listen to tapes of conferences, counting particularly important features, then, like researchers, offer an interpretation. They can take turns acting as observers as they watch pairs of students or teacher-student pairs wrestle with revising a text or constructing an interpretation of a literary text, again, paying careful attention to issues of gender and language just as they have observed differences between conversation and teaching. They can observe videotapes of students and teachers confering so that they have access to paralinguistic cues as well: body language, eye-movment, and facial expression. And they have access to all sorts of language interaction taking place around them at home, work, dorms, restaurants, etc. Identifying high-stakes, asymmetrical interactions and considering how gender is affecting those interactions leads to an awareness of language and gender as shaping forces in the outcomes.

Much of what we hear in conferences we respond to unconsciously, and in many ways, much of what we say is also not open to reflection, at least at the moment. If teachers have adopted a strategy of taping conferences, students and teachers can revisit those tapes to study and analyze their own language, just as we revisit written texts to understand what "worked" and what was less successful. After having students participate in some of their own research, I found that they were willing to listen to what I offered in terms of my conferences. Women especially were struck by and concerned with the use of " I don't know" and negative self-generalizations. As a class, we have spoken about conferences in relation to interviews, where the assessment aspects are more clear to participants: the possible outcomes of negative self-generalizations, or of putting forth ideas without any indication that other possibilities exist. Students, aware of the power relations and high stakes that can be part of a conference, begin to see language and gender as linked in a larger structure of power relations. Who will get the job? Who will have access to money and power? Who will get praise and help? Who will have access to knowledge and other members of the community? And, of course, what does entry into that powerful community mean for each person?

Just as we cannot dismiss our power as teachers, we cannot shrug off our genders and the ways in which we have learned to perform them. But that does not mean we cannot understand the dynamics of language and power, nor does it mean that we cannot alter them once aware of them. As teachers who have chosen to conference in order to help students and to shift what seems to us to be a sometimes unhealthy relationship, we need to do whatever we can to accomplish those goals.

CHAPTER FOUR

Cross-Cultural Conferencing

A LINE OF POETRY FROM ADRIENNE RICH BURNED ITSELF INTO BELL hooks's memory and life.

> "This is the oppressor's language yet I need it to talk to you." Then, when I first read these words, and now, they make me think of standard English, of learning to speak against black vernacular, against the ruptured and broken speech of a dispossessed and displaced people. Standard English is not the speech of exile. It is the language of conquest and domination; in the United States, it is the mask which hides the loss of so many tongues, all those sounds of diverse, native communities we will never hear, the speech of the Gullah, Yiddish, and so many other unremembered tongues.
>
> Reflecting on Adrienne Rich's words, I know that it is not the English language that hurts me, but what the oppressors do with it, how they shape it to become a territory that limits and defines, how they make it a weapon that can shame, humiliate, colonize. (1994, 168)

* * * * *

Ben finished telling me about his plans for writing the upcoming paper. Then, before I could speak, he leaned forward and in a rush of words beginning with "because," he justified all that he had just told me, earnestly supporting each of his arguments. Perhaps I had drawn one of those breaths that said I would challenge him; maybe I squinted my eyes in one of those I'm-not-entirely-convinced-of-this looks. Or maybe Ben assumed that whatever he said would be challenged. He anticipated a Wh- question (Why? Who? What?) and didn't even wait for me to ask it.

I had begun to study my own conferences, and I noted as I transcribed my conference with Ben that neither of the other two males had anticipated any challenge to their ideas. The women had, however. Ben was the only African American in the study. Was his justification based on some cue from me? Or was it based on a personal history of challenges by teachers?

I couldn't answer that. And that made me uncomfortable, not just because as a new teacher I thought I needed to have all the answers, but because Ben's response to me (and perhaps mine to him) had highlighted for me how ethnocentric my training had been, how segregated my life experiences were. I grew up in southeastern Massachusetts at a time when the largest minority population was the Portuguese, who had come first to work on the fishing boats and later worked in the cranberry bogs. I'd gone to primarily white schools, lived in primarily white neighborhoods, though certainly some of them were working class or lower, and now taught at a university that was primarily white and middle- to upper-class. While my own working-poor cultural background had made me feel apart from the usually wealthy students I taught, I still felt I "knew" their culture and values. Nowhere in my life had I really thought much beyond socioeconomic class as culture. And certainly, nowhere in my three-week teacher training course or in the year-long mentorship that followed had the issue of cross-cultural communication been spoken of. We had been given advice on grading, book selection, paper assignments and writing a syllabus. I understand now that any training is a luxury most teaching assistants don't experience. I understand the focus on logistics, on "trench work." But choices indicate values and beliefs, and not only was talk between teachers and students considered unimportant, but talk between teachers and students from differing cultures was even less emphasized.

At a recent conference, a teacher from Kansas told us that in her school district, 42 different languages were spoken by the students. Along with those languages come cultures and sets of beliefs. Statistics on population growth and change predict that by 2020, whites will no longer be the majority population in the United States (Banks, 18). As our classrooms become more diverse, the chances for miscommunication become more frequent. Consider something as simple as the words "okay" and "yes." Deborah Tannen (1982) reminds us that when we hear a familiar word seemingly used in a familiar way, we will interpret it according to our culture. But in her study of Greeks and Greek Americans, she found that while for Americans "okay" is an affirmative response, for Greeks and even Greek Americans, it is used as an unenthusiastic response, agreement without enjoyment. There are more, subtle differences that can be confusing. "Why" can be either a request for information (American perspective) or an "indirect way of stalling or resisting compliance with a perceived request (Greek perspective)" (223). Tannen tells us that Greeks value "enthusiasm and spontaneity," while Americans value planning and organization. For Americans, brevity indicates "informality, casualness, and sincerity," while for Greeks, it is "a sign of unwillingness to comply with another's perceived preference" (228). It is easy to imagine a conference in which an American teacher makes a number of suggestions to a Greek student for planning and organizing an essay or revising an earlier one and receives an "okay" in response. The requests for planning or organization may run counter to the student's cultural response to an assignment to write, and her response, seen as affirmative, is really unenthusiastic. What may result is an essay that does not meet the teacher's expectations as the student instead approaches the task in a way that seems more "natural" to her; the teacher may feel as if the student has misled her, has not been fully honest about her unwillingness to follow the well-intentioned advice.

Experience will have taught a great deal to those of us work daily with large numbers of students for whom English is not a native language, speakers of Black English Vernacular (BEV, also called African American Vernacular English or AAVE), and students who are bilingual and/or perhaps come from a culture different from the mainstream. Some of us have our roots in those "non-mainstream" cultures. But a great many of us work with only a handful of such students at any given time or find ourselves suddenly in a situation where our culture and language are different from most of our students.

> It is a sharing of conversational strategies that creates the feeling of satisfaction which accompanies and follows successful conversation: the sense of being understood, being "on the same wave length," belonging, and therefore of sharing identity. Conversely, a lack of congruity in conversational strategies creates the opposite feeling: of dissonance, not being understood, not belonging and therefore of not sharing identity. This is the sense in which conversational style is a major component of what we have come to call ethnicity. (Tannen, 1982, 217)

It is this dissonance that many teachers mention when they speak of conferences with students who are, in some ways, "unlike" them. What happens when we don't feel as if we belong? When we don't have a sense of being understood? Or when we simply assume we are understood? What happens when it becomes clear that we are mis-communicating, but we are unable to understand why and seemingly unable not to keep talking at each other in the same ways? It's like the old slapstick routine where a speaker, told a listener doesn't speak his language, simply repeats himself but louder this time.

Language and Culture

When we are in our culture, firmly a part of it, it is invisible to us. Only when I stepped out of my working-class culture into the upper-class culture of my undergraduate institution did I see how the ways that I spoke, dressed, and thought both made me a part of where I came from and set me apart from my new community. I was a silent student for years, reticent in the dorm conversations, quiet and obe-dient in my work-study jobs, a non-participant when floor mates talked about vacations, family jobs, career connections, and travel experiences. I read, I listened, and I studied how they spoke and acted. I learned in an English class that Huck Finn couldn't imitate a woman successfully because he'd never had to study them, never had to respect their power and control. But, my teacher posited, a woman could have impersonated a man—the oppressed culture always stud-ies the oppressor. I remember the males in the class laughing and shifting position to sit with their legs demurely crossed, speaking to each other in falsettos. We all laughed, but I realized that's what I'd been doing—studying my college classmates so I could impersonate them. Clothes I could pick up at second-hand stores; I could make up stories about family or experiences or brush off such questions. But I was having difficulty with the speech. For a long time, silence was my only hope of disguise.

Until recently, the study of interethnic or cross-cultural commu-nication has been largely the domain of anthropology, and certainly not a part of literature and composition. The canon has only now begun to shift to include writing by non-mainstream authors, and only in the last two decades has the shift to process-oriented approaches to composition allowed teachers to better understand the ways in which students from non-mainstream backgrounds must shape their writing to produce the most desirable aspects of Standard Edited American English. And with the exception of Black English Vernacular, most of the research has focused on cultural differences in writing, not speech. But our experiences as teachers and students tell us that we judge and are judged on the basis of many characteristics, and when one group has the power to define, evaluate, and place—to control effectively for many years, sometimes for a lifetime—the academic and life-path of members of another group, serious consideration ought to be given to the criteria by which those judgements are made. One of the ways we judge is by speech.

What do we predict for our students as we first meet them? As we read their essays? As we hear how they respond to a question? As we observe how they are dressed, how they seat themselves in the room? As we notice racial, ethnic, or cultural characteristics different from our own and all the beliefs we struggle with or against come into play? William Labov noted, as have many other linguists and sociolinguists, that speakers of non-standard dialects have an immediate strike against them, for listeners immediately and negatively judge their intelligence and sometimes their honesty (1972). Victor Villanueva (1993) writes passionately about the denigration of African Americans on the basis of their language, summarizing research and "findings" of cultural deprivation and low intelligence. "'Round and 'round she goes. Since the question always is 'What's wrong with them,' the answer gets repeated too: bad language equals insufficient cognitive development" (11). And he reminisces about his kindergarten teacher's attempt to rid him of his accent; she urged his parents to speak to him in English, not realizing that he had learned his accent from his parents, who only spoke with an accent *because* they spoke English (32). She apparently did not misunderstand Villanueva, but his accent was a reminder of his otherness, something he could hide by speaking properly. The ridiculing of Black English Vernacular, of Ebonics, of all non-prestige dialects, the fear and fervor that fuels the English-only movement, continuing calls for separate nations, and characterizations of affirmative action as "reverse discrimination" are sonar images of the deep channels of racism and ethnocentrism that lie beneath shallow democratic waters. There is nothing special or extraordinary about Mainstream American English or Standard Edited American English. What's special is the power, the status of those who speak and write it. They have the power to proclaim that it's what must be spoken and written or the social consequences will be devastating—imagine: people who *can't even* speak English will be running the world. It's a vicious cycle: if you can't learn to speak English you must be dumb; if you're that dumb or don't *want* to learn then you shouldn't be in a position of power and authority. Hell, you shouldn't even be in the country.

So much needs to be said, to be addressed, to be brought out into the open, to be discussed. But many teachers discover that when they try to create a dialogue in their classrooms about issues of race or ethnicity, about minority and immigrant experiences, about class, students are reluctant to discuss them. Some students believe so firmly that classrooms are places of absolute equality that they will not taint this safe place by having such a discussion. Other students discover that they do not have a vocabulary to discuss race and racism that is not racist. Some feel inequity doesn't exist—there is nothing to discuss. Some are so angry about the injustices they have suffered that they fear to give voice to that anger. And rightly, many don't understand why they must discuss what the teacher wants them to discuss, what the point of this all is. They know that it will be an "academic" discussion, that the directions they might wish to take it will be closed down, that it will result in nothing tangible. Unless action accompanies speech, unless learning and transformation are the outcomes of discussion, it is just another exercise in the name of multiculturalism. "Critique alone is an inadequate response to actual human suffering" (Bruch and Marback, 278). And those who are "other" than the academic mainstream often have suffered greatly. Cross-cultural teaching and communication is "messy" and that the traditions of education in this country don't allow for or "appreciate" such messiness. So we respond by "cleaning up" the mess. How many times I've heard teachers tell their students to "clean up" their writing, as if error—sometimes merely difference—was dirty.

> When student writers bring with them different languages, discourses, cultures, and world views, the culture of the academy would leech out their cultural uniqueness, absorb them, assimilate them, graduate them uniform in their uniforms. Admittance requires conformity and the attendant cultural loss...as language can be the great equalizer, so can it be the great nullifier. (Okawa, 1997, 98)

Yes, yes, we tell students, your language is valuable. We are not so explicit in telling them: But I'm not going to learn it, you're going to learn mine. And until you do, your essays will be graded as poor and your speech will mark you as a non-member of this community. And when you no longer exist as "other," as what you are now, then we will embrace you. That's suffering.

When issues of cultural difference and dominance remain muffled in the classroom, why should we expect it to be any different when we move to a conference? Lisa Delpit (1988) brings us the words of a Black woman, a doctoral student and school principal.

> Then, when it's time for class to be over, the professor tells me to come to his office to talk more. So I go. He asks for more examples of what I'm talking about, and he looks and nods while I give them. Then he says that that's just my experiences. It doesn't really apply to most Black people.
>
> It becomes futile because they think they know everything about everybody. What you have to say about your life, your children, doesn't mean anything. They don't really want to hear what you have to say. They wear blinders and earplugs. They only want to go on research they've read that other White people have written.
>
> It just doesn't make any sense to keep talking to them. (281)

Delpit goes on to widen the scenario.

> One of the tragedies in the field of education is that scenarios such as these are enacted daily around the country. The saddest element is that the individuals that the Black and Native American educators speak of in these statements are seldom aware that the dialogue *has* been silenced. Most likely the White educators believe that their colleagues of color did, in the end, agree with their logic. After all, they stopped disagreeing, didn't they? (281)

I read Delpit's article not long after I began to study my own conferences. It was given to me by a colleague who worked in the writing center, a place where student tutors, unlike teachers, spoke openly about the cross-cultural difficulties they'd experienced. The vast majority of tutors were white, middle- to upper-class students, usually female, and their clients were African American or international students. My colleague was educating herself about the politics of conferences, for the tutors believed that because she was a T.A., something closer to a teacher than they were, she must know some magic way of bridging those differences. How would she? This is not something we usually talk about, for it highlights the gulf between races in this country, and the dominance of one particular view, one set of standards. A Black teacher tells Delpit that she cannot talk with her White colleagues, for "they listen, but they don't *hear.*" From the classroom to the writing center to the individual conference, we are often speaking at odds when we speak in a multicultural setting. Without a set of shared assumptions or knowledge of each other's cultures, both parties in a conference will feel dissatisfied, frustrated; we will have spent time in a place where we did not belong.

Hearing and Not Hearing

As I considered and reconsidered what I was communicating in this book, I knew I wanted to write about cross-cultural differences. But in the tapes I had available to me, there was largely an astounding match, a similarity in race and class between students and teachers. As deeply imbedded as I was in this project, almost hyper-sensitive to language, I did not want to tape my own conferences with students whose cultural or racial backgrounds differed markedly from my own, knowing I would be more careful to shape my responses. So I recently asked colleagues for new tapes, and one offered me three. The first was with Uri, a male student from Ossetia, a small country in the Caucasian Mountains in Russia, where the native language has ties to Farsi but the official language is Russian. The other two conferences were with female students from Japan, Yoko and Miko. The teacher himself is not a native speaker of English; Hamid is from Iran but has lived for many years in the United States. And so in this chapter, we will not hear the words, the voices of many "others," those students who are so often silenced in so many ways in our educational institutions. The irony of this is not lost on me. But I am uncomfortable speaking for them, and have in some ways lost my own voice in this chapter, deferring to those who have more experience in this particular aspect of teaching and conferencing. In my first draft of this book, this chapter didn't exist. But I wrote in the introduction that I had given myself permission to ask questions that I had been afraid to ask before, and this chapter is the result. Many of us may be afraid to ask something like, "But how do you conference with Native Americans?" It's too close to saying, "How do you conference with *them*?" It is frightening to admit to such ignorance and ethnocentrism. But to ask the question opens up the door for understanding how the structures of our culture encourage such isolation, even in a field where supposedly the goal is to make everyone equal and equally educated.

Hamid told me that his conference with Uri, the Ossetian, was not typical—it was too conversational and there were no difficulties. Uri's understanding of English was excellent—he even extended an analogy made by Hamid. He was able to write humorously, and to understand another culture's humor is to have a good grasp of the culture. So I chose not to use this conference in this chapter. But Hamid found his conference with Yoko a bit more typical. "Plagiarism is something I have to be constantly on guard about with ESL students. Writing is tough for [them] and sometimes they make it more difficult for themselves by being too concerned about getting it right in the first draft. Thus, the tendency is greater for ESL students to 'borrow,'" he wrote on his response form. Certainly, plagiarism happens among all groups of students, but another cultural difference is the idea of "owning" ideas. We adhere rigidly in the United States to the divisions between "common knowledge" and individually "owned" knowledge. For students from many other cultures, if the material is printed and thus commonly available, then why shouldn't it be used? Once they read it, it becomes part of their knowledge, in the same way that most of their ideas and beliefs have come initially from external sources— as have ours. It may also be a gesture of respect to embed the words of an authority in your own—respect for the writer whose work you felt was important enough to use and respect for a reader in the effort to provide the "best" information or text. But in the United States, we respect "originality" and mark the origins of work.

Hamid asks his students to read aloud several samples of their work when they conference with him. After Yoko reads a new journal entry on a recently opened computer lab on campus and receives praise, Hamid asks her to share with him the revisions she has made on an earlier piece of writing. I have tried, where possible, to transcribe exactly the pronunciation of student and teacher, because those are the "voices" that were present in the conference. Hamid's accent is quite subtle, often just a change in vowel sounds, while Yoko's is more pronounced. Because much of the conference involved the student reading her work, I transcribed only exchanges between the teacher and student. Thus, line numbers begin anew with each segment of interaction.

001 Hamid: Uhkay. Very good. Ahm this is the one from da last time?
002 Yoko: Yes. Aaaht-
003 Hamid: ⌊Okay.

004 Yoko: I totry.. changed introduction? A:nd you say you don't understand dat
005   us and dem teory so I just gi- could add example?
006 Hamid: Okay.
007 Yoko: A:nd yeah pretty much I- compretely changed introduction, and I-..
008 Hamid: Changed that par⌈t
009 Yoko: ⌊Give more information about dis part and I jus-..
010 Hamid: Ch⌈anged
011 Yoko: ⌊Checked checked the gramma:r mist⌈ake and this kind of thing⌉
012 Hamid: ⌊/uhm/   ⌊So you
013   make those minor s- those minor ⌈modifications.
014 Yoko: ⌊Yuh.
015 Hamid: Okay. And wha: dese what are these, ah
016 Yoko: Oh. Dese were the fur- final ones.
017 Hamid: Ah⌈kay.
018 Yoko: ⌊I went to s- uh Writing Center?
019 Hamid: Uh ahk⌈ay.
020 Yoko: ⌊To get the I needed help?
021 Hamid: Ah good! Well I'm glad you did that.
022 Yoko: (softly) Yeah.
023 Hamid: That's goodt.

After checking on some unfamiliar markings on her paper and discovering she has gone for sanctioned assistance, Hamid asks her to read her first two paragraphs (the second one is quite long) to him. She agrees, but warns him that "First, le- introduction is totary changed, so." She goes on to read her first paragraph, which tells readers that the Japanese speak little and rarely express their feelings or opinions strongly or directly, but it doesn't mean they don't pay attention—it's simply a cultural difference. She expands on an earlier idea: the "us-and-them" theory. She reads her second paragraph, which explains in more detail how the culture has isolated and pro-tected itself. The language in this paragraph is anthropological, and the syntax is graceful. She struggles to read parts of the essay.

001 Hamid: Okay good. Now dis is very nicely ⌈done, it is definitely explains the idea of
002 Yoko: ⌊(Softly) mm-hmm
003 Hamid: ⌈us-and-them very clearly. Oo:, oowhat do you mean by "tacit?"
004 Yoko: ⌊Mm-hmm   Ta⌈s:
005 Hamid: ⌊Tacit
006   understanding.
007 Yoko: Like... it's- there's a /common/ in between us.. lik⌈e, there, uh, yeah.
008 Hamid: ⌊Mmm

009 Yoko: (2.5 sec) Like you don't have to say a word. Like.⌉
010 Hamid: ⌊Mmm
011   Did you get these ideas from a book or an article or something?
012 Yoko: I: get dis... from deh uh wait a minute. OH! I called my.. parents so I
013   went- ⌈call--
014 Hamid: ⌊Yeah. Yeah. Bwhen you talk to your parents you talk in Japanese,
015   ⌈is dis/ right? But some of the sentence structure and vocabulary here,⌈it
016 Yoko: ⌊Yeah   ⌊Yeah
017 Hamid: right? But some of the sentence structure and vocabulary here, it does not
018   sound like your style.⌉
019 Yoko: ⌊O:h
020 Hamid: (2 sec) Eah, I'm just wondering you know whether you were influenced by
021   somebody's writing.
022 Yoko: ⌊Ah, what de- de difficult words I think I get from⌈ the dictionally?
023 Hamid: ⌊Yeah
024 Yoko: Like I know the Japanese difficult words and den when I look da dictionally
025   dat saying dis kind of difficult word look like--
026 Hamid: ⌊But did did you read someting
027   before you wr- wrote this because, ⌈THERE'S EVIdence that you were..
028 Yoko: ⌊Yuh, I WROTE, I- wh-
029 Hamid: directly influenced.
030 Yoko: ⌊Yes, I-   read da uh aricle yah in Japanese.
031 Hamid: IN Japanese. ⌉
032 Yoko: ⌊Yeah. ⌉
033 Hamid: ⌊But, eh, how about in English.
034 Yoko: I don't have in Japanese so, some.. Japanese sentence I jus transrate to
035   English by myself, so..zer's no such uh aricle in English, ⌈but I HAVE some
036 Hamid: ⌊Okay (softly)   ⌊Mbut there's lots
037 Yoko: ⌈aricle--
038 Hamid: ⌊in English, yuh. ⌉
039 Yoko: ⌊in Japanese.
040 Hamid: (very softly) Mm-hmm
041 Yoko: Talk about us-and-dem teory?
042 Hamid: Ahkay. (2 sec) Aahright. (4 sec) Uhkay let's go on to the next essay
043   please?

The audiotape registers a tightness, a higher pitch in Hamid's voice in the final line of this excerpt. He is clearly concerned about plagiarism, and tests her ability to explain some terminology. Yoko repeats with some difficulty a definition in her paper, and when questioned about where she got material, she announces after some hesitation and almost as a discovery that it came from her parents. Hamid becomes more specific, and Yoko says that yes, she read articles in

Japanese and translated them. At no time does she say the ideas are her own; even as she attempts to answer Hamid's initial question, she begins with "I get dis from de uh...." She seems confused by Hamid's assertion that there are indeed articles about this theory in English, for she appears to be referring directly to the articles she claims she had in her possession when she wrote, none of which were in English. She has read and understood them, responding to his request that she explain more clearly a concept she had raised in an earlier draft.

Yoko explains to Hamid that she has changed her topic for her second essay from a doll festival to a discussion of New Year festivities in Japan. When Hamid asks her why she changed her topic, Yoko explains that she could not generate two pages of material. She has no freewriting to accompany the new draft, but Hamid asks her to read through her essay anyway. Again, this essay employs complex syntax and some sophisticated diction that the student stumbles over. After she reads, Hamid asks her to do some freewriting for 10-15 minutes. When the tape resumes, he asks her to read her new work. This time, there is a great deal of repetition in the syntax—Yoko uses the words "New Year" in almost every sentence, and while there are still some longer, more complex sentences, many more are short and choppy. Hamid asks her to describe the differences between the two drafts. Yoko points out that she had completely left out the introduction and written what she wanted to; given a chance, she'd go back and put an introduction in later.

This isn't the only paper Hamid has received this time about the Japanese New Year.

```
001  Hamid:  And then a few things that you do on New Year's Eve such as eating this
002          special food and watching TV.
003  Yoko:                 ⌊Food     ⌊Yuh
004  Hamid:  Which are pretty much what ea:h what's her name, uh Miko wrote⌈about,
005  Yoko:                                                                  ⌊Yes
006  Hamid:  you remember? Yeah. So then it seems to me ⌈you were a little ⌈influenced
007  Yoko:                                             ⌊Mm-hmm     ⌊I yeah I
008  Hamid:  ⌊y her.
009  Yoko:   ⌊totary forgot about her writing though.
010  Hamid:                                  ⌊Yeah.
011  Yoko:   /Da bells?/
012  Hamid:  Uhkay.
013  Yoko:   And I- uh after I
```

014 Hamid: Yeah⌉
015 Yoko: ⌊/look/ I read her ⌈story. Y⌈h. That also.
016 Hamid: ⌊Yeah. ⌊It seems to me that what you have
017   written here (referring to freewrite) is very different from what you gave
018   me at the beginning. Isn't it?
019 Yoko: Oh! The k- the begi⌈nning? Da firs⌈t free write?
020 Hamid: ⌊Yeah   ⌊Dis first di- this one ⌈h
021 Yoko: ⌊Ah yes.⌉
022 Hamid: ⌊Yeah.

The free-write includes information on the usual events of the Japanese New Year celebration, but it is missing the historical commentary that bracketed the draft she first presented Hamid. Yoko doesn't expand on any of the differences she sees, and Hamid doesn't ask her to. Instead, he asks her to write another draft, working directly from the free-write done in his office and forget completely about what she first presented. He asks her to provide him with a series of drafts showing exactly how she gets from the free-write to the finished essay he will see later. Yoko agrees, but returns to the historical material that she wants to include.

001 Yoko: But in this first write uh freewriting I don't have definition I don't have like
002   definition of da new⌈ears, so when I wro⌈te da first essay, I: got da definition
003 Hamid: ⌊Uh-huh   ⌊(Very soft)okay
004 Yoko: of da new ear ⌈what dey used to do? In.. like ancient like, ⌈where I come from
005 Hamid: ⌊Uh   ⌊Yeah
006 Yoko: wh why we start cerebrating the the new ears, and den I- got the
007   information about ancesnors? And like, we- but I didn't know dat before,
008   before I... ⌈get da full information about our new ears. And I got it and den
009 Hamid: ⌊Wrote dis
010 Yoko: jus transrate it (laughing) ⌈by myself, like..⌈I got da definit⌈ion..
011 Hamid: ⌊Mm-hmm   ⌊/?/   ⌊So I'll I'll write
012   here then what you need to do. Develop- this is what you want to do,
             ⌈ight? Write on this one.⌉
013 Yoko: ⌊Mm-hmm   ⌊Yes.
014 Hamid: Develop this draft (Sounds of writing heard)
015 Yoko: Mm-hmm
016 Hamid: And then take it to the Writing Center.
017 Yoko: Okay.
018 Hamid: (2 sec, writing) and get feedback (3 sec, writing) Keep a record of
019   everything, uhkay?
020 Yoko: Okay.

021 Hamid: (writing) Keep a record (2.5 sec, writing) and then eahm, eahm, revise..
022   And te- show me all drafts... I'm gonna ke- make a: copy of this one, and
023   keep a copy of the first one you gave me and we have agreed that this will
024   be a completely different essay.
025 Yoko: Mm-hmm. Okay.
026 Hamid: Uh-huh? Great. Thanks a lot. Do you have any
027   questions?
028 Yoko: No, I don't.

To any experienced teacher—and quite probably to most American students—Hamid's final instructions are clearly designed to prevent this student from plagiarizing and to support any case he may make in the future regarding her "misconduct" in using outside sources. Yoko seems somewhat aware of Hamid's concern, as she raises the topic herself, telling him that she translated some sources to provide information in her first draft. But she seems to have the concept that since *she* was the translator, the words are now hers. Her laughter and insistence that she got the definition may imply that she is proud of her work in developing a new essay.

Why didn't Hamid just talk with her about plagiarism? Why didn't he tell her directly about his concerns? Curious, I asked him. He told me, angry still that Yoko had plagiarized, that he didn't need to, it was "implied, it was understood." He wrote on his response sheet that this student was really a "capable writer" but she "wants to boost her grade with minimal effort." He makes it a rule to not talk about plagiarism with a specific student unless he is prepared to "go the whole route," following the university guidelines for dealing with plagiarism. He handles the issue delicately, not only because of the complicated institutional procedures he might put in motion but because "you don't want to say what you don't know." He pointed out that she didn't challenge his implication; had she done so, he would have had to be more forceful, more assertive. He didn't even believe, he said, that the journals she took the information from were Japanese, for she did not have the English skills to translate the Japanese into such graceful and lengthy English sentences.

Certainly, the change in style marks another "voice" in the two essays, and like Hamid, I am convinced that the writing is not her own. But Yoko's lack of challenge does not necessarily mean that she has understood the unspoken, her breach of one of the foundational tenets of western academic writing. She seems proud of her new knowledge about her own culture and about her ability to develop her draft in such a way that her teacher more fully understands a concept she wants to explore, that, in fact, he asked her to say more about. Indeed, speaking in a way she herself says is rare in her culture, she asserts loudly and over Hamid's questioning that she DOES have these articles in Japanese. And she seems to want to restore to her essay the historical information Hamid wants her to forget about. She translated it herself, she got this information. She doesn't challenge Hamid enough to make him become more forceful in his charge, but little in her response indicates she understands exactly what lies behind his concerns. Her repetition of "I got the information" implies that, rather than concerns about plagiarism, she may think Hamid believes she is fabricating information. At the time this chapter was written, Yoko had not yet resubmitted her essays, but it would not be surprising to me to see the disputed material reappearing in the next version as well.

Talking with Non-Native Speakers

Ulla Connor (1997) reminds us that "cultural mismatches manifest themselves in several classroom situations: conversation, collaborative groups, and student-teacher conferences" (206). Unfortunately, research on differences in writing skills—as opposed to speaking patterns—between non-native speakers of English and native speakers has received the most attention. Tony Silva (1997) summarizes the results of a number of such studies which included speakers of 17 different languages. On the whole, he reports, the writing of ESL students is judged to be "simpler and less effective" by NES (Native English Speakers); their essays are "shorter, contain more errors...and their orientation to readers was deemed less appropriate and acceptable." They were, overall, less "sophisticated" (215-216). Villanueva points out that studies on the written prose of Spanish speakers, including such diverse cultures as Ecuadorians, Puerto Ricans, and speakers of Mexican Spanish, found longer sentences, a tendency toward the abstract, stronger reader-writer interactions, and logical connections between sentences that weren't immediately apparent to native English speakers. There was also more repetition and "ornateness" in prose by these writers than prose by native speakers of standard English (85). Such differences mean that in collaborative groups, many peers spend time working on surface features with the writer rather than ideas and issues. The same can happen in conferences. For example, when Hamid and Miko, another Japanese student, conferenced, Hamid asked a question about *osechi*, food cooked and stored in multi-leveled containers and eaten throughout the Japanese New Year celebrations. Miko responded by describing the container; again Hamid asked about the food and again Miko returned to the container. Hamid persisted, explicitly asking not about the container but the food, and she responded this time with some additional details: fish, eggs, vegetables in a sauce. Perhaps in her culture the two—food and container—are not separable? What might be only an aside in a conference with a native speaker becomes time-consuming, and time is usually in short supply for conferences. Curiousity, even niceties, may have to go by the wayside.

The differences in writing styles also mean that many ESL students spend significant time in writing centers and in conference with their teachers, being taught conventions they may not fully understand. Villanueva remembers the comment "Logic?" being written on paper after paper, even in graduate school. His Anglo friends could not explain to him how his thinking differed from theirs, and he would not ask the teacher. "To ask would be an admission of ignorance, 'stupid spic' still resounding within. This is his problem" (73). Does Yoko understand plagiarism? Hamid planned on a general discussion in class soon after his conference with her; he said that the one or two students who were plagiarizing would know it was directed toward them. Perhaps given the indirection that is part of Yoko's culture, Hamid's approach will both save face for students and teacher and help his class learn. But it is a difficult concept even to explain to American students.

How well do teachers and students understand each other's cultures?

> Japanese and Chinese tend to be more indirect that Americans; Finns and English speakers have different coherence conventions, the Finns leaving things unsaid that they consider obvious and the English speakers expecting them as clarification; and Korean students do not want to take strong positions in defending...decisions. (Connor, 207-208)

Muriel Harris (1997) reports that ESL students from various countries shared a common belief that it is a teacher's job to lecture, while tutors discuss. It is the teacher's job to evaluate, to point out problems, but a tutor's job to offer specific help, to answer questions (223). For many ESL students, then, the conference is an extension of their own classroom experiences, where they are passive learners; active learning takes place with peers only. Teachers who challenge that role may find themselves met with silence. And she reminds us of an Asian custom of making friends before getting down to business. In tutoring situations, that means some friendly "chat" before tackling the task at hand; such "chatting" was rare in conferences I listened to, and usually took place only *after* the task was completed. Lisle and Mano (1997) highlight a Vietnamese cultural tradition that interferes with communication in conferences. In this tradition, children, even those who are over 18, are expected to remain silent, for only adults can express opinions (14). Harris points out that European students as well as those from Pakistan are used to being formally addressed and may take offense at the teacher's use of their first names only. At every turn, if we are paying attention and asking questions, we will see how the many assumptions we make about communication do not hold across cultures.

Even the smallest words or gestures can be misunderstood. Susan Fiksdale (1990) studied "gatekeeping" interviews between foreign students and international advisors—professors who were charged with making sure both that students were making academic progress and had taken all the steps necessary to remain legally in the country. The term "gatekeeping interview" refers to situations where the interviewer "actually holds conflicting roles: acting as a guide as well as acting as a monitor of progress for an individual's career" (4). Concerning herself with "timing"—the right word or gesture at the right time—she discovered that the Taiwanese students she was studying frequently offered backchanneling (*yeah, uh-huh*) without an accompanying nod. She points out that "saying *uh-huh* without nodding only occurs during uncomfortable moments for native speakers" (7). The disruption this caused in the timing of the advisor's speech resulted in the advisor stopping to offer a hyperexplanation, assuming that the student was confused or had misunderstood him. When Fiksdale asked students about their use of words like *uh-huh, okay, yeah,* and *yes,* they reported some confusion about how to use them. One telling comment: "I don't know the proper word to say in English so I just..try to find some word say-if I come out with say *yes* that's no problem. I won't say *no* ((laugh))(double parentheses Fiksdale's) it keeps the communication going" (2). Whether he understood his advisor or not, what was crucial was to keep the conference going. Both Fiksdale and Harris comment on the importance of "face" and "saving" or protecting face. In order to save face, Asian students may say they understand something even if they don't; in face-to-face interaction of all kinds, not solely cross-cultural, the need for "orderly communication" and the preservation of everyone's face takes precedence (Fiksdale, 57, citing Goffman, 19). When Hamid asks Yoko if there are any questions, she says no. She never asks why she must abandon a more fully developed draft for her freewrite, and Hamid does not elaborate. Perhaps, like me, she heard the anger in his voice; perhaps she understood that if she pushed him to explain, everyone's face would be in danger of damage. After all, it is not his job to discuss but to lecture.

If we imagine (and some of us have experienced this) a mainstream teacher conferencing with a student from Taiwan, we might see the teacher speaking at even greater length than usual. Prompted by repeated positive backchanneling (*yes, uh-huh*), the teacher continues talking. When her student nods at a time that seems inappropriate, the teacher may stop, backtrack, and explain again. The student may respond positively when the teacher asks him if he understands now; he may or may not actually understand. When the teacher stops and asks the student why he wrote a particular sentence, she may receive, after much prompting, a response that seems indirect, that "begs the question." Frustrated, she continues. The student asks some questions, but most of them are about lower-order concerns: punctuation, spelling. At some point, the student begins to speak a bit more, perhaps beginning his turn with *so*. What a teacher might see as summarization (*so*) would be a new topic for an ESL student; the misunderstanding may mean that the teacher does not take up the topic, instead framing it in her head as "sayback" of what she has already told the student. When the teacher does not respond "appropriately," the student does not offer the topic again, for to do so would result in negative face for both participants. The teacher begins again, marking that with *now*. An ESL student may not realize that *now* is signaling a new topic for the teacher, and may continue to frame this new information under the umbrella of the earlier information, thus misunderstanding partially or entirely the new topic. Some misunderstandings may be worked out later in the writing center, where the student feels more comfortable asking questions, but many will remain unresolved.

Black English Vernacular and Writing Conferences

Hamid heard an admission of guilt from Yoko. Without the anger of the teacher facing plagiarism, with the time to read and reread transcripts, I heard confusion. When I turn back toward my own conferences, I have to ask: was I hearing my student Ben or just listening? Was I making it clear to him in all sorts of ways I didn't realize that I wasn't hearing but was already judging, evaluating? What kind of damage do I do when I enter into a conference with a student and know nothing of her culture, her beliefs, don't attempt to understand the nuances of her language but impose mine instead? I thought back to Delpit's passionate article again when I began counting words in my research, listening for Lily in her conference with Nina—the woman who had worked in the writing center. Lily agreed with everything Nina said. She responded briefly but courteously, offering no more than "Okay" or "Yes." Perhaps, as bell hooks writes, Lily is following the African American rule: "keep your stuff to yourself," be "private...about your business" (*Talking Back,* 2) And yet, teachers sometimes encourage students to talk about themselves and their lives; they ask questions that deal with the student's town, home, family, academic experiences, and current situation in school. (They don't always share that information about themselves with the student, however.) But people who have lived lives under scrutiny, who have had to answer questions that violate their privacy, who are aware of how such information may be used against them or may be used to fill in blanks in a stereotype, may need to protect themselves, may see such questions as probing, aggressive, and unnecessary to accomplish the task at hand—improve a paper. And, if the shared cultural context between teacher and student is limited, how much of that information will be understood in the way the speaker wishes it to be?

Lily was religious, Nina told me, and was always quiet in class and conferences—she wished she spoke more. When person A says person B is religious, it often means that person B is more religious than A; a point of difference. Nina valued participation highly and defined a key aspect of participation as speaking up appropriately in class and conferences; Lily's level of participation disappointed her. Even though she did not see Lily's silence as belligerent or impolite, it was still a negative. She did not consider (at least in talking with me) that it might be deference to her authority as a teacher, or that it might represent Lily's accurate understanding of the great gulf that separated her from her teacher. Perhaps Lily's speech, like her written text, included aspects of BEV, and she knew that such non-standard speech would be viewed negatively. Which is riskier: to speak and reveal something a teacher may respond to negatively or not to speak and have the teacher see that as a lack of enthusiasm? While the images of African Americans we see through the media are becoming increasingly more diverse, the emphasis on negative images for speakers of BEV is still present.

The characteristics of Black English have been well described. Most teachers are familiar with the way Black English Vernacular's use of the copula ("to be") and marking of plural differs from Standard English or, as some researchers prefer, Mainstream American English (MAE). The presence of these items alone in an essay are usually enough to have students placed in remedial classes, sent off to writing centers, or summoned to conference with a teacher. But there are other less immediately noticeable differences from Standard English. The rhetorical structure may also be problematic for teachers used to clearly stated thesis statements and linear development rather than circumlocution, and the clear acknowledgement of sources rather than the borrowing and weaving together of ideas. Bonnie Lisle and Sandra Mano (1997), summarizing cultural differences in rhetoric, note Geneva Smitherman's (1986) descriptions of several BEV features: "call and response," where listeners offer active vocal support for speakers; "signifying," when a speaker slyly and often humorously chastizes another person; and the ways in which indirection in speech and a pattern of circumlocution help the speaker "stalk" the issue and ultimately persuade listeners. Denise Troutman (1997) emphasizes the participatory nature of Black English, the ways in which the speaker attempts to involve the audience, "pulling it into the linguistic event" (29). Repetition is also an important part of BEV, perhaps an influence from African American preaching style. Verbal styling, playing with words and rhyme, the twisting and turning of ideas is highly admired. Kermit Campbell writes of BEV speakers' fondness for extended, deeply-layered metaphors (1997, 93). Marsha Stanback (1985) points out that the "braggadocio" of BEV speech is not limited to African American men. "Smart talk," or signifying, loud-talking, and braggadocio, is one of the most "outspoken" styles of speech for Black women; they are as proficient as men (182-183).

One of the values bell hooks finds in BEV is the way that historically it has served to shape a sense of community among African Americans.

The rupture of standard English enabled and enables rebellion and resistance....The power of this speech is not simply that it enables resistance to white supremacy, but that it also forges a space for alternative cultural production and alternative epistemologies—different ways of thinking and knowing that were crucial to creating a counterhegemonic worldview. (171)

Despite hooks's joy in the promise of BEV to challenge white, upper class control, this rich linguistic heritage finds little space in most classrooms. In traditional classrooms, teachers are not "brought into" a student's speech. Students respond, they do not perform. Students answer directly, not with indirection. Play with words in speech is often seen as "showing off" and wasting valuable time. Many teachers do not see how this indirection, this verbal turning of ideas parallels the ways in which traditional essays turn and twist and consider an issue from many perspectives. Teachers may hear BEV directed to classmates as the speaker involves them in his answer to a teacher's question, or they may hear it as a student complains about a grade, comment, or assignment, not to the teacher but within her hearing distance ("sounding off").

But many teachers will not hear this verbal style spoken directly to them; speakers of BEV are much less likely to use their vernacular in institutional situations and with white speaking partners. Rebecca Moore Howard (1996) asserts that "AAVE (African American Vernacular English) has no public life in American society. It is a private language of one group" (270). In a course about language, race, ethnicity and history, the largely African American class voted to have an AAVE day, where all would speak in that language. But when the time came, of 28 students, only two and Howard herself actually used AAVE. White European students felt to do so would be to "mock" their African American classmates, and African Americans feared that they would "appear ignorant." She argues that "AAVE [is] a private code sometimes witnessed but never spoken by outsiders, a private code never spoken out of context. Code switching *to* AAVE is profoundly constrained" (270).

Knowing that BEV has no prestige and conveys a negative image, most African American students will "code switch" when conferencing with teachers. That takes some concentration, especially when a student is also being asked to use a new, disciplinary language as well. Rather than "slip" and begin speaking in a way that is comfortable and familiar, rather than further set themselves apart as "other," one strategy is to respond minimally. In doing so, the student can focus on what the teacher is saying—it's a wise learning strategy. But in not responding as "fully" as the teacher may expect, the student is also not doing all those things that teachers are looking for: engaging themselves with the material (and the teacher!); demonstrating by repeating back to the teacher that they have been listening and understand this new information; indicating a willingness to develop the writing using their own ideas. It is a double bind.

But even listening closely may not be of much help. Lisa Delpit highlights the differences between middle-class, mainstream teachers' style in giving directives and the way directives are given in African American culture. Indirection—"Do you want to open your books now please?"—and statements phrased as student desires, not teacher demands—"You want to avoid doing that"— contrast with "Open your books now" and "Don't do that." Delpit informs us that

> Black people view issues of power and authority differently than people from mainstream middle-class backgrounds. Many people of color expect authority to be earned by personal efforts and exhibited by personal characteristics....Some members of middle-class cultures, by contrast, expect one to achieve authority by the acquisition of an authoritative role. (289)

Members of the Black community respect a teacher who exhibits personal power, believes in all students, reaches out to students to create close personal relationships, and "pushes" students to learn (Delpit, 290). They are explicit about their power and they use it explicitly to help their students. Michelle Foster (1995) studied the ways in which an African American teacher wove elements of BEV into her class and responded to student expectations for teacherly authority. Her students, largely African American, respected her. "She's a damn good teacher because she gets to the point of the conversation, is direct, and aggressive, which are signs of leadership and is why I take her seriously" (133). The teacher was also aggressive in exploring with her students the kinds of oppression, the social and economic structures that had so often negatively affected their lives. Lisa Delpit quotes white teachers who shake their heads about the authoritarian teaching style of an African American colleague, while not realizing that their own style conflicts with those same students. Many mainstream teachers hide their power; they do not display it openly but expect students to understand their "suggestions" as orders because a suggestion from a person with power IS an order. This difference can lead African American students to misunderstand the desires of mainstream teachers, to see suggestions as options, not demands, to believe that the teacher who does not "run" a class lacks the knowledge, skill, or desire to do so. This lack of respect in the classroom can translate into a reluctance to follow the teacher's suggestions in a conference. It can also lead to confusion as mainstream teachers "suggest" ways of revising or hint that a sentence construction or an interpretation is "problematic." If a mainstream teacher speaking Standard English tells a BEV speaking student "You might want to change your approach to this issue," for the teacher it clearly means, "Change it." The student may or may not hear that command. If she asks, looking for clear direction, "Does that mean you want me to change this? How?", the teacher may become very uncomfortable: she has been asked to make explicit the power she has tried to mitigate. Such cultural and language differences mar the often "seamless" surface of conferences and remind participants that things are not always was they seem.

Class is Culture, Too

We don't like to think about it this way in the United States, the "classless society." My students say fiercely, regardless of class, "Some people have more money than others, so they can have more things. But that doesn't mean they are any better than a poor person." The bootstrap doctrine, the belief in equality is so strong that many people have difficulty seeing how culture and economics play out in a country that Martin Luther King Jr. pointed out was founded not on democracy but capitalism. Not until college did I begin to understand it myself. It took awhile for me to realize how many activities I couldn't participate in because I worked on weekends and some evenings in the library; how many clubs I couldn't join because of activity fees; how many relationships I would never have because I couldn't afford to share the same experiences as many of my classmates. I remember feeling desperate and singled out when a teacher commented with disdain on my use of onion-skin paper, the only thing I could afford. I borrowed typewriters and could type only when one was available, since I couldn't afford one of my own. I've already described the ways in which those class differences played out in conferences. From the sting I still feel as I list these differences, I remember how hard it was to lose those cherished beliefs that had sustained me as I grew up. And I fought hard to keep them.

Twenty years later, I watched as an elementary school teacher in a southern Ohio classroom wrote on the board a sentence that resonated with the Appalachian dialect of many of the children. This sentence was "clearly wrong," she told them, and asked how it might be made "right." A student whose clothing and speech marked her as middle class and less "provincial" corrected it on the board with the teacher's repeated approval while my niece turned to me and whispered in anger and some fear, "Mamaw talks like that!"

Our students feel those class differences. They are acutely aware of how we signal our class, from clothing to gesture to language. But for lower- and working-class students, what seems so valuable and important to them at home is worthless in a school environment. Lisa Delpit puts it this way:

> I have frequently heard schools call poor parents "uncaring" when parents respond to the school's urging, that they change their home life in order to facilitate their children's learning, by saying, "But that's the school's job." What the school personnel fail to understand is that if the parents were members of the culture of power and lived by its rules and codes, then they would transmit those codes to their children. In fact, they transmit another culture that children must learn at home in order to survive in their communities. (286)

Shirley Brice Heath's (1983) work on language use in two communities highlights how class differences in language cut across racial boundaries. Children, both black and white, from the working class and working poor misunderstood the language of their middle-class teachers. Coming from households where clear directives were the norm, they responded slowly or not at all to the implied directives of their teachers. They brought a rich oral tradition, a joy in community speech that conflicted with the traditional classrooms. Their parents, too, had difficulty understanding what teachers wanted from their children. People in these two working-class/working-poor communities saw the world holistically, learned in context, not by separating out objects from one another. Much of what we do in school is to separate something from its context—an idea, a word, an object, an issue—and examine it, compare or contrast it to something else. In mainstream academic culture, understanding something discretely rather than holistically has been the norm. When asked to separate, to distinguish one thing from another or to make analogies, children either did not respond or did not respond "appropriately." The fragmentation of knowledge modeled in the mainstream, middle-class classroom was foreign to them. The clash between "home language" and "school language" is also a clash between cultures, values, and ways of seeing the world.

Bell hooks asserts that, after a dozen years of being prepared for college, "students in public institutions, mostly from working-class backgrounds, come to college assuming that professors see them as having nothing of value to say, no valuable contribution to make to a dialectical exchange of ideas" (149). Those "twelve years of preparation" separate children into those who may speak and those who ultimately may not—and sometimes cannot. In a several year study of minority children, Ray Rist (1970) observed how class differences, even at the kindergarten level, translated into an impoverished academic life. He followed a group of African American children through the second grade, making formal and informal observations, interviewing the teachers, talking with the children, and visiting their homes. He gathered data on their families, activities, and expectations, and charted the interaction between students and between students and their teachers, all African American. The results of his study, though two decades old, remain very disturbing. Within eight days of the start of kindergarthen, the teacher, with no standardized test results but with access to her students' personal files, organized her students into three groups, each of which sat at a single large table. The first group, comprised of children she expected to succeed, were seated at the table in the front of the class. These children met "prestige" standards: they spoke easily with the teacher, using standard English more often than not; they were more likely to come from homes with two parents with at least high school and possibly college education; they had a low number of siblings; they were less likely to be receiving government assistance; their clothes, even if not expensive or new, were clean and mended; they arrived with their hair brushed, and had no offensive odors. The remaining two groups were organized by how closely they fit these characteristics, with children demonstrating the fewest number of them at the last table, table three.

As Rist followed the children throughout the first year, he noted that the children's involvement in classroom activities was directly related to their placement. The teacher provided information mostly to the first table, directing commands and orders for behavior more often to the other two tables. She chose students to speak more often from the first table, selected students from that table for coveted "jobs" in the classroom like leading the pledge of allegiance, and put them in positions of authority over the other children (appointing one "sheriff" during an outing).

The children from table one clearly understood their higher status, for they often called the other children "dumb" or "stupid," and chided them for their inability to do some of the assigned tasks (although the children at table one had received direct instruction in those tasks, unlike the other children). Even students who sat at those two rear tables labeled themselves negatively, and began to show hostility toward each other, though they didn't show it with the higher status children. Visiting the children in their homes, Rist saw that children from tables two and three *were* learning, though they had little chance to prove it in class. They learned from listening to other children actively participate in lessons; they studied their classroom materials at home.

At the end of the school year, "objective" standardized tests "proved right" the teacher's initial evaluation of her children's skills: students scored well largely in direct relationship to the tables they'd been assigned to. Children from tables two and three were labeled "at risk" and again put at tables where they received less instruction, more control, and more criticism. Rist followed this group of children for two more years. A few students originally placed at the second table moved up to the status of those at the first table, but by and large, that first judgment of the children's abilities, based solely on markers of class, held firm in the school system.

Rist describes a situation where the effects of language and class are potentially devastating; that is, he describes a classroom. But in a classroom, at least, misery has company. In a conference, the individual student may feel on trial, even if the teacher doesn't realize it. How does class play itself out in a conference? To be "wrong" when you open your mouth is a frightening thing. I've written of my own silence; because it remains so close to me I've worked, through making a personal connection, to create a safe place for my "lower class" students to speak with me. I remember an office partner turning to me after such a conference and saying, "You'd think by now he'd have learned not to say 'ain't.' That drives me crazy." In a system based on ranking, on evaluation, students who are already low-ranked societally fear that their failings will be magnified in open interaction with a teacher. All of us misunderstand sometimes or find ourselves confused by terminology or ideas. But if you have been placed at the third table for most of your academic life, if you have not had a chance to use the language you heard addressed to others or have had little assistance in applying techniques or gaining skills that are necessary for advancement in status, you may well need more time to process rarely used or unfamiliar vocabulary or suggestions for improving an essay. Unless a student in this situation gives the teacher some indication of confusion (and unless the teacher creates such an opportunity for the student to speak!), the teacher may think the student is a lot of things—sullen, withdrawn, quiet, shy—but will probably also assume she understands what is being asked of her. Why ask the teacher, if doing so will underscore your stupidity? Your low status? When the paper comes back, the teacher will know anyway, but why invite such an evaluation now? Moving between classes is not easy; there are still times when I must search to translate what I really want to say into a language that will be accepted and understood by my faculty or administrative colleagues.

Native American Cultures

While most Native Americans are native speakers of English, many may be bilingual, and many have grown up in a culture that differs from the mainstream in significant ways. Their language patterns reflect those cultural differences. My husband was interviewed by telephone for a position as an archivist for the Dakota Sioux. He was very qualified, he felt, and approached the interview with enthusiasm. I left the house during the interview to give him the space and quiet he needed. When I returned, he was depressed, not sure what he had done wrong. He said it was the most awkward interview he had ever done. There were long silences, and the interviewers said little to him. Rather than blather on, he said, he had fallen silent himself, and nothing but static passed across the phone lines. He was sure he'd lost the position. Later, after he was hired and had lived on the reservation for some time, he learned that silence after a speaker's turn indicated respect. After all, the person may have something more to say, for not all our thoughts come out at once. It was linguistic space, an opportunity for the speaker to move the talk to a deeper level. There was plenty of time for other speakers to join in as they wished, and perhaps they must gather their thoughts together, changed now by what had been spoken previously. He learned that his decision to be silent himself had played a positive role in his being hired.

Michelle Grijalva, addressing the oral tradition of many Native American tribes, encouraged her Native American students who felt ashamed of their speech

> to understand silence as an effective rhetorical tool that gives shape to sound and meaning—not to confuse it with the inarticulate and illiterate or with the inchoate place of nonbeing, a void that lends itself to shame and insecurity. Rather, the silence of storytellers can remind us that there is such a thing as the unspeakable, something we might call the silence of the sacred, or it can simply signal an inappropriate time to speak. Storytellers teach us that silence is the beat and pulse, the rhythm keeper of the oral tradition. Storytellers who are not afraid of silence can hold their audiences; they are the survivors. (1997, 48)

The oral tradition of the Native American Pueblo culture has similarites to BEV in that communication is considered to be a communal act, where the speaker draws the story out of the listeners. It is a language of connectedness and inclusiveness, with stories leading to each other in a weblike fashion. The traditional thesis and support structure, the linearity of mainstream narrative would not allow for such exploration, such connection (Lisle and Mano, 17, 19).

Often, in writing assignments or conferences, we invite or ask students to write or speak about their personal experiences. Judith Villa (1996) points out, however, that for many Native Americans, such a topic is taboo or inappropriate (246). The personal experience is always part of and less important than the communal experience. In her experience teaching, tutoring, and conferencing with Native Americans, she found that her students would not come to conferences or tutoring sessions if they were set up by her. Instead, they followed a pattern described by Roland Tharp, Stephanie Dalton, and Lois Yamauchi (1994), who argue that "most native students are more comfortable and more inclined to participate in activities that they generate, organize, or direct" (37, quoted in Villa, 256). Villa found that her students would come around if she was available; that they would "hang around" for a long time to see if she was equally committed to communication, and finally begin to talk with her, though always indirectly about whatever was the issue. The need to establish connections, to see academic material as part of a larger context, was fundamental to success for the students.

Not understanding Native American culture (and of course it is not monolithic; there can be significant tribal differences) can lead teachers to ask students to write on topics or in a way that clashes with cultural beliefs. Villa recounts two stories which are illustrative. A Native American student was asked to critique a student art show, but instead wrote mostly about his own art. It was not part of his cultural beliefs to criticize others in the way the teacher suggested. While he felt he fulfilled the assignment by critiquing his own work and then comparing it to what he saw in the art show, this more subtle approach earned him a "D." Another Native American student, a Navajo woman, struggled with an assignment to write about "A Rose for Emily." Traditionally, the Navajo do not speak of the dead. It would be easy for a teacher, even in conference, to miss the reasons behind the "failure" of these two students. Remember Mary asking Rick about his dead grandfather? To question the Navajo student about the text, about dead relatives, or about issues in the same domain that are part of this piece of "American" literature would be offensive, and the student response would be as silent, as noncommital as the paper this student eventually wrote. All the parties understand the words, but they attach different meanings to them. Breaches of important cultural beliefs and unfamiliarity with cultural speech patterns doom conferences to time spend in a mire of cross-cultural misunderstanding.

What We Can Do

It will take more than simply "celebrating diversity" to make the fundamental changes needed to truly respect the languages that each of us is competent in. When we tell students that their home languages are valuable but make no space in the academy for those languages, we force them "to move back and forth between a privatized dignity of difference and a public dignity of sameness and assimilation" (Bruch and Marbach, 275). We cannot "know" all cultures, but we can begin by educating ourselves in two directions, which will eventually cross paths: we can acknowledge and respect the diverse cultures around us and we can study (not just live in) our own. For many of us who teach, school IS our life. But it is not, by and large, our students' lives.

To study ourselves, we need to consider those moments when we have experienced "otherness." For many of those in the mainstream, those are painful moments, experiences we have tried to bury—lives unmarked by otherness is the norm. My sense of otherness when I entered college has stayed painfully close to the surface; like many of those from the working class or the working-poor levels, I sometimes feel like an imposter in academe. I remain convinced that one stupid comment, one naive response to a colleague will be enough to blow my cover. But usually I am in control of academic language, if not academic knowledge. Being thrust into another, foreign language culture can remind us what it feels like to not belong on a most fundamental level—speech. On a trip to Miami to speak at a conference, I found myself surrounded by Spanish speakers, and stood silent, unable to enter the conversation. When hotel clerks spoke in "asides" in Spanish, I felt momentarily angered, as if somehow I was *entitled* to know what they were saying, entitled to the respect they would show by speaking my language at all times. A little disoriented, trying to figure out my reactions, I went to the beach to sit and read. A man came up to me, smiled, pointed at the sea shells I'd collected, and made a comment in Spanish. I shook my head. He stared at me in amazement. I managed to stutter out some version in Spanish of "I don't speak/understand Spanish" (which I'm pretty sure I picked up from a police drama where the officer was responding to the Hispanic "perp"!) and he shook his head and walked away with a little smile. I felt and was dumb.

I have felt otherness when I sat as a graduate student in a committee meeting of all male tenured faculty members. And I have felt otherness as I simply walked through a largely Black urban neighborhood. But all of these have been fleeting experiences, and I could always retreat to the privilege of my whiteness, or my status as teacher, or as a member of *at least* the lower middle class. I have not experienced many of the kinds of otherness I've written about in this chapter. Simply acknowledging that is a start. And another small step—admitting that when I did feel some sense of that otherness, I wanted not to be like those who seemed so different from me but instead wanted them to be like me, or at least not try to make me be like them. To understand the need to retain culture, heritage, and language in the face of pressure to assimilate can provide a teacher with compassion and understanding.

To be not just critically self-reflective but also self-revelatory is also crucial. Educator after educator who works extensively in cross-cultural situations stresses the power of narrative to bridge gaps, to create connections. Stories can be compared, contrasted, interrogated, and retold without attacking or questioning the teller. There are, after all, multiple narratives for every event. We accept all the stories of eye-witnesses as true in some way, shaped by their point of view, their past experiences, their relationship to the teller, the event—their historical, cultural, and institutional positions. My experiences with schooling will be different from my students. Why? Critical analysis of stories begins to clarify the constraints and privileges of our individual lives. We learn from stories—if we listen to them, if we encourage them to be told.

I have already discussed elsewhere the authority of the storyteller. It is a power that can be shared. And as students find themselves telling their stories, sometimes in their own language or at least partially in their languages, as they find themselves teaching others and see the merging of private and academic language, they begin to question what is so prestigious about Standard English, how it came to be the "standard" by which they are judged now.

Many minority educators argue that we must be explicit about power and codes of the powerful, about what is expected and what the outcome of not meeting those expectations are. When we articulate those expectations, there is at least the possiblity that they can be questioned, that we ourselves will begin to question and examine them. And when we ask, "How are these expectations different from what you do/think/believe" then we begin a dialogue on culture that can potentially create the conditions necessary for students to empower themselves, to make choices with knowledge and awareness, to effect some change. What if Hamid had asked Yoko about her use of sources, about her beliefs and then shared with her his own? What Hamid does do, however, is to summarize the main points of the conference and write down for each of his students explicitly what he expects them to do before they meet again. As he lists each process or change, he speaks with a questioning tone not indicated in the transcripts, inviting students to ask for any additional clarification.

Everywhere in this book, I've argued that classrooms and conferences are closely connected, that whatever we hope to accomplish in our conferences is dependent upon how we shape our classrooms. If real exploration of culture and cultural difference is not part of our classrooms, then culture will become an undercurrent in conferences, sucking in the unwary. Just as research on gender differences can become part of a classroom, so can research on cultural differ-ence. In writing classrooms, studying what students choose to write about or how they approach a topic helps us understand different rhetorical traditions and can help both peers and teachers under-stand how to respond to writing. Teaching our students and our-selves to ask why a student chose a particular approach or a construction, not simply rushing to point out that it doesn't follow standard English conventions or sometimes even the assignment, is far more instructive and opens up spaces for dialogue. Sharing with a writer our honest responses to writing that is not mainstream helps writers understand the effect of their work on others, and, if we examine our responses, helps us understand our own cultural beliefs and values. Encouraging students to speak in their home languages as much as possible and to clarify or translate what is not clear to lis-teners can help create a classroom where language is freely shared and issues of competency are highlighted: if listeners cannot under-stand a person speaking fluently in her own language, who then is competent and who isn't?

Most of us have the power to select the texts that our students will read, and our choices will reflect what we feel is most important, most valuable to our classrooms. Teachers know that students learn best when we present new information in ways that relate to their experi-ences. Yet the texts we choose and the ways in which we present them are often distant from the lives and knowledge of non-mainstream students. I remember struggling through long novels that took place in parlors; not a single novel moved me until I read *McTeague.* Then I dove into the literature of Realism and Naturalism—books that fea-tured characters familiar to me (but often in ways I could authorita-tively criticize). Only then could I go back to those earlier parlor novels with some ability to analyze. Additionally, texts that offer stu-dents alternative rhetorical patterns to the mainstream ones that so often fill classrooms also provide the opportunity for non-main-stream students to see their language and culture centrally and pos-itively positioned. Black educators have written of the struggle to teach African Americans to value BEV in texts; Michelle Grijalva writes of the sense of shame and resistance she initially encountered when she brought Native American texts into her class of Hopi and Navajo stu-dents. "American" literature, narrowly and Eurocentrically conceived of for generations in academe, can be studied from many ways of speaking and seeing. This means using whole texts, not simply readers. Many students are completely put off by the complex messages being sent by the "multicultural" readers that are part of so many well-intentioned liberal classrooms. Sandra Jamieson (1997) points out that the selections in such readers continue to support the status quo, continue to position women and people of color as "other" and as victims even as they propose to "celebrate" diversity. Standards for writing are clearly delineated, yet when the writing of women and people of color are held up against these standards, they fail. Texts by writers from a variety of cultures and languages which examine the same issues or events are particularly helpful in bringing to the forefront the ways in which language and power are connected.

In conferences, students from such a classroom would not only be able to speak with authority about the texts they are reading, but would be able to speak fluently, using their home language as much as possible. Instead of minimal responses, instead of face saving, teachers and students would be more likely to engage in a dialogue. Here, in the conference, where most students receive the only individual help the teacher can offer, discussions of how their language use differs from the standard would be informed by a more mutual understanding of the cultures that give rise to difference and the power structure that turns difference into issues of dominance.

Sociolinguists assume that all communication is meaningful. As teachers, we need to learn to ask not just ourselves but our students "Why?" Mina Shaughnessey (1977) gave us this lesson again and again as she studied the writing of her "remedial" students, those "Others" the university had been forced to admit. With each choice of a word, each selection of a piece of punctuation, a student writer is constructing writing that is purposeful, is revealing knowledge both common and idiosyncratic. And we are lucky that we do not have to figure out this sometimes-puzzle alone—we have the student, the writer herself to ask.

CHAPTER FIVE

The Affective Dimension

Through our talk about things, we sustain the reality of them. We are choosing what parts of the world we will orient to, and we are defining what aspects of reality are most important. The question of who controls topics in our conversations is partly a question of who controls our view of the world.

P.M. Fishman, "What Do Couples Talk About
When They're Alone?"

I LOVE TEACHING. I LOVE TO READ BOOKS, I LOVE TO READ STUDENT papers, and I love to read, period. As a undergraduate, I "hated" *Portrait of a Lady*, but I "loved" *McTeague.* T.S. Eliot and Wallace Stevens interested me, but Robert Bly, Sylvia Plath, and William Stafford moved me. I was embarrassed by my writing in an introductory fiction class, to the point where I still remember most of what I wrote and how shallow and awkward it seemed next to my more talented classmates' work. I felt proud and special in my poetry workshops, loving this poem, frustrated by the next, but feeling talented because my professor told me he liked what I wrote.

I am talking about feelings here, about emotions that mingle with factual knowledge. Most of us who have gone into teaching have done so because there is something about it that we love; there is some need it fulfills. And while some may conference with students because it is required, most of us conference because there is an affective dimension to teaching and learning that is important to us, and conferences seem to be one way to address that dimension for ourselves and our students. We come into conferences feeling something about this student, something about the texts at hand, just as our students come into conferences full of feelings. And when we ignore this dimension—as I believe we so often do—we miss what prompted our students to write or what kept them from writing what they wanted; we miss developing the trust that comes from sharing feelings as well as facts and writing strategies; and we are frustrated by what has remained unsaid, unexplored, or unresolved.

In the long and frustrating conference I taped with my student, Felicia, the important issue became her feelings: her fears about writing and about how I would respond to her as a student and a person. After I had questioned her into a corner and she stammered out that she didn't "know how to say things," it was clear to me that she didn't understand the revision strategies I had suggested, didn't understand the point of my asking these questions, didn't understand where I thought I was leading her. I was thinking there was some particular kind of knowledge that was hidden in her head like cached treasure and that I could trick her into revealing it or help her remember the way back. Then, voila! I would "see the light in her eyes," and we would make this wonderful paper together.

"I don't know how to say things." What a courageous admission to make to someone who so values exactly that knowledge! I remember how her voice shook and how she tried to make a little half smile and then turned away. Everything in her tone and body language told me that she was not asking for another lesson on how to say things, though she would have been happy for me to tell her exactly what to say at that moment and end the torture. We were talking about a lifetime of humiliating conferences and comments on papers; Felicia was afraid and anxious and knew the stakes were getting higher with each class, each year of school. Yet I didn't want to deal with it nor did I have the time to do so. For Felicia wasn't the only student who needed something from me, and we'd already used up our twenty minutes. So I resisted the way she had suddenly begun shaping the conference, resisted speaking, too, of my own fears of having the wrong words years before and even now. I told her quickly a few things she should do to improve her paper, thanked her for coming, and sent her on her way. Ignoring the topic she had offered, I told her, in essence: "This is the academic world, Felicia, and it doesn't involve feelings, particularly student feelings. Get over it." I place my conference with Felicia in my column of worsts; I am ashamed of using my power as teacher to silence Felicia and tell her, in ways subtle and not so subtle, that her feelings didn't count, weren't valid, didn't even warrant acknowledgment.

Students Say. . .

When I've asked students to write about their best and worst conferences, it's clear that the emotional aspects of a conference play an important role in their choices. Students are afraid, nervous, excited, or uncertain about themselves and want to talk about those feelings, want to establish a relationship with the teacher that goes beyond the classroom. One student described how he felt when his teacher bracketed conferences with personal questions.

> He'd begin by talking about the area that I live in, and since he, too, has been to the Washington, D.C. area, he could relate to me in that aspect. I think by talking about something totally unrelated to English I was able to relax more, and feel like this teacher who I had a conference with was my good friend....After we were done talking about the papers, he continued to talk to me further about other things I am interested in, like baseball. I think by talking about these things helped me to respect my teacher and his ideas, and to feel like he was my friend instead of my teacher who I was conferencing with.

Another student writes that she came from a small high school and feels the "need to be noticed." She seeks out conferences with her teachers, especially in classes in which she is doing poorly. "I have found that those conferences have helped the most, if not in learning the material then just to relate to the teacher and ask questions. I feel that these conferences are quite helpful and often give me better confidence and more interest in class." Clearly, the goal for conferencing can be either or both writing/revising a paper and establishing a relationship with the teacher that is comfortable for the student. One student is willing to forgo learning course material in order to "relate" to the teacher, for her confidence in her ability depends upon her relationship with that teacher. Another student wants her teacher to talk a lot—but in very particular ways.

> A good conference is when the teacher does a lot of talking—makes you feel comfortable. Many times when I go to see teachers I am very nervous. When they are friendly and outgoing I feel more comfortable and can discuss my problems. Many times they act cold and I find myself just wanting to hurry and get out of there ASAP. I can't be myself and I don't get my problems solved. All teachers seem to intimidate me.

When we talk about writing without talking about feeling, we abstract a set of skills and a string of words from what has been a personal process, a human connection. What makes certain memories of conferencing so strong for me is not whether I got the advice to rewrite a particular paper and get a good grade, but whether I felt welcomed or humiliated or valued or threatened. I don't ever recall a teacher asking about my feelings, being concerned about my confidence or fear. They might have been, but there was no space to talk about those feelings, or perhaps neither of us knew how to make that space.

Discourse and Affective Topics

As I examined other conferences, I explored topic change and kinds of topics. I divided them into broad categories: discourse topics were primarily about writing, affective topics primarily about feelings (and in these conferences, that often meant feelings about writing), and a category of "other" topics, most of which dealt with the surface of the conference or a course—when papers were due, what changes had been made in the syllabus, etc.— made up the rest. Teachers, who controlled conferences generally, not surprisingly also controlled topics. Their topics were primarily discourse ones; for teachers, feelings are usually expressed only in the form of either praise or criticism. They are firmly part of teaching, barely different from the discourse topics that make up so much of conference talk: "I really like what you've done here," "I remember feeling badly when I gave this [paper] back to you in class because I should've said that about the central metaphor the first time around." Even for students, feelings were rarely offered unwrapped, naked. Instead, they were clothed in concerns about what the teacher wanted or liked. When students did offer up their feelings as possible topics, teachers found it difficult to respond to them, to help students articulate or explore those feelings. And in the case of a teacher who expressed personal feelings about his job with a student, the student was not in a position to respond as an equal, was not prepared to bridge the gap between teacher and student, between classroom and colleague.

Mary and Rick met to talk about Rick's paper, which Mary had found so vague and unfocused that she requested the conference. Rick has had a great deal of difficulty with a poem, and as the two worked their way through the poem, they came across some coined phrases: one in particular, "wanwood," stopped them.

168 Mary: I never heard of wanwood
169   but I thought it was just because I was (2 sec) not very educated

170   (Laughs).
171 Rick: I never heard of a lot of em, but.. I guess I'm not educated either.
172 Mary: Well
173 Rick: I shouldn't be here, what am I doing here.
174 Mary: Oh, that's not TRUE! (Laughs)
175 Rick: Sound like Scott now. ⌉
176 Mary: ⌊WELL, if he's gonna be makin up
177   words, you know, I mean he has⌈to expect people to feel those
178 Rick: ⌊To explain em, right?
179 Mary: things, right? Okay, so we have a sense, general, vague, maybe
180   but a sense--
181 Rick: ⌊I don't even know why I picked this poem, I was⌈just--
182 Mary: ⌊You don't
183   know why. ⌉
184 Rick: ⌊I was just looking through it.
185 Mary: It's--
186 Rick: It caught my eye.

For Rick, this task seems overwhelming. His frustrated exclamation that he doesn't belong here seems to imply not just this conference about this poet and poem, but "here" in the university generally. Mary refutes his self judgement, Rick compares himself to someone else they both know, and Mary goes on to offer her support for Rick, pointing out that Hopkins should expect people to feel this way as they approach his creative language. It's interesting that she doesn't address Rick's concerns directly, but shifts the focus to the poet. She might have said, "It's perfectly natural to feel as frustrated as you do; you're dealing with lots of new information at one time, not just in this class, either." Instead, she asks Rick to think about the poet, not himself. With her one sentence, she feels she has responded to his affective topic and shifts quickly back to the discourse topic, marking that shift with *Okay* and a summary of what they've accomplished in the minutes before this. But Rick's frustration hasn't been addressed, and he interrupts her to reassert his topic. This time, she is more aware of the depth of his fear and frustration, and helps him develop his topic more fully. Rick goes on to say that, coming from Canada, he would have had one more year of school before entering a university, would have read different authors before dealing with these. He's not sure that having missed that year, he was prepared for school. But she is still intent on getting through THIS poem, and again, she tries to shift the topic.

227 Rick: See if I woulda gone back to grade thirteen we woulda had to do
228   Frankenstein. In the thirteenth grade this year.
229 Mary: O:h. The- there were thirteen grades in your school? In your
230   high school?
231 Rick: Yeah. In Canada, you have to go thirteen grades.
232 Mary: O::h.
233 Rick: It's like first year university, so.
234 Mary: A:h. We::ll, you missed something there. So I guess what we
235   have to decide, you have to decide first is which poem do you
236   wanna use.

Rick goes on to begin to develop a paper idea, but his sense of being overwhelmed re-emerges near the end of the conference. He wants advice on how he should start his new paper.

376 Rick: Dyou have to be, be creative?
377 Mary: (Laughs) Do you have to be creative?
378 Rick: (Little laugh) I don't wanna be creative now.
379 Mary: Well, I think you--
380 Rick: ⌊Everything- Everything's goin on,⌐/ ? /
381 Mary: ⌊I know, there's a lot
382   going on, life is very tough these days.
383 Rick: An we're always doing something with the /hockey⌐team/
384 Mary: ⌊Do you
385   have a um, a computer, or are you using a typewriter.

Rick's worries about time management, his own skills, his fit with the school all underlie this conference. They keep resurfacing, and despite Mary's attempts to deal with them quickly, they will not go away. For Rick, his feelings about school and his ability to succeed are clearly more important than the necessity of writing a paper. At the end of the conference, as Mary is attempting to get him to commit to finishing the paper soon, he brings up his grandmother's gallstones and her hospitalization—he has already told Mary how important his family is to him. His feelings run like a cross current that constantly threaten to pull the conference in a direction that Mary does not want to go.

Not only students but teachers bring with them feelings that affect the shape of conferences. But because of the power relations, students find it hard—if not impossible—to ignore the affective topics that teachers raise. Because they cannot leave and must respond, students can find themselves in a situation that calls for sophisticated skills. Don is frustrated with his students, frustrated with the pressure of earning a Ph.D. and the conflicts between teaching and his own writing and work. He cares deeply about his students and his teaching, he cares about his studies as a doctoral student, and he also works many odd hours to make a living and support his education. His weariness and anger is as much a part of this conference as—if not more than—his student's paper and her questions.

As the conference opens with Lyn, he dismisses the importance of the conference he has just completed taping and admits that he is self-conscious about being taped.

```
01   Don:   Hope I have as much fun with this as I had with the first one
02          blah blah blah blah /and on/. (Lyn laughs) Ye:::p (makes noise
03          like he's stretching) Okay. Well (2 sec) I always feel dorky about
04          being on tape, but--
05   Lyn:                     ⌊I know. I had to do this for my tutor, too.
06   Don:                                                        Did ya
07          really?
08   Lyn:   ⌊I had t'be on a video camera.
```

They go on to talk about Lyn's experience being videotaped, and perhaps because she has been sympathetic toward his discomfort, Don reveals something that he and his office mate, Sue, have discussed in private.

```
17   Don:   We've talked about in here many times an an Sue
18          will attest to that about y'know just when we always sit
19          around n bitch about what our students are like (Sue laughs,
20          maybe says something inaudible) an what how we would like
21          our students to be and we and we always say gee we oughta just
22          like play the videotape you know record this and then show it
23          to it to our students so they know exactly what issues er y'know
24          what axes we grind about them (Sue or Lyn laughs) so that they
25          can you know can sorta think about that uh for the next class.
26          U:m
27   Sue:   Oh they would just die if they knew what we (somebody laughs)
28   Don:   They'd no of course but I mean students talk about their
29          instructors I mean so we may as you know we may as well admit
30   Sue:                  ⌊/ ???/
31   Don:   that we talk about our students.
```

```
32   Lyn:   Well I don't see why you wouldn't.
33   Don:   Well I think it's a necessity. So⌈ um... Well but but it would be
34   Lyn:                                      ⌊Mm-hmm
35   Don:   good just t'know y'know just some a the y'know the issues that
36          are out there for us as teachers that's all. But I think it would be
37          st strange I think we'd be we'd be all very self conscious like I
38          am right now about this being recorded or filmed. (5 sec)
```

A few turns later, Don rereads his comments on Lyn's paper and confesses that he read it at two-thirty in the morning and couldn't really give it a "thorough shakedown." Don's frustrations with his situation arise again when he instructs Lyn to speak directly into the tape recorder and share with me her opinion (which he supports) that the student guide to first-year composition is useless, knowing that I played a large role in that year's edition.

In the competition between Don's anger and Lyn's concerns, Don's frustration takes precedence and Lyn's concerns about her paper and her questions often go unanswered, receive contradictory answers, or provide more opportunities for Don to explode again. When Lyn tells him that this paper was hardest to write because for the other papers, "all you had to do was an analyze what you read n n spit it back out," Don responds: "Yea:::h everyone says that. That's right n I get tired of reading things that people spit up on a paper." Both then laugh, but Don's anger, like Rick's sense of inadequacy, continues to erupt.

As Lyn searches in her folder for a different paper to discuss, Don yawns and sighs. When Lyn tells him "You ripped on my grammar /and things like that/", Don is taken by surprise.

```
314  Don:   Huh?
315  Lyn:   My grammar /?/
316  Don:   Did I hammer ya on that?
317  Lyn:   Oh yeah (laughs).
318  Don:   (2 sec) Well I'm hammering everybody on that. I'm probably gonna use
319         Elements of Style next.. semester in 111 just cause I
320         think it's
321  Lyn:   I don't think I was ever really taught any of that (laughs) and if
322         I was it was something we breezed over. Cause I as I think that's
323         how I write
324  Don:   You know I I haven't come up- uh across any paper that I'm just
325         bored to death with that I think are you know (2 sec) completely
```

326 devoid of any intelligent thought but... some a these things get
327 so:: bogged down and..some a these things get so bogged down
328 with bad.. writing an fractured syntax that it uh it's u:h I just
329 sorta throw the paper down I can I can't read that shit. (Lyn laughs)
330 I I I get frustrated by /bad sentence structure/
331 Lyn: ⌊I'm sure this is probably one of them.

Lyn directs his attention to the second page of her paper, where Don reads aloud his comments, sighing as he does so.

339 Don: (Turn continues) This may have been like the twentieth
340 paper I read that day (Lyn laughs) so I mean that's you got the
341 worst of it. I probably this is you're probably you're payin in this
342 for all everybody else's sins before you.
343 Lyn: (Laughs) I just started laughing because I knew it was true.
344 Don: (3 sec) Yeah. Well that's it's a good satire there I mean it's not
345 too (2 sec) Oh now this is not satirical this is this is real (2 sec)
346 U::h Oh you (sounds like he's stretching) I dunno what to do
347 well side from the mechanical things an the stylistic flaws..I
348 think it's a good paper. (7 sec, seems to be going through pages and
349 reading, humming) do do da do:: do do ta do do ta do::...
350 so what's your question on this?
351 Lyn: Oh. (Sounds suprised) I dunno. What are what are stylistic
352 flaws?
353 Don: Well this whole matter of of .. sentence fragments uh use of s of
354 uh y'know use of a semicolon where you should have comma
355 (2 sec) U:m
356 Lyn: (3 sec) Basically mechanical writing.
357 Don: Yeah an sort of well yeah generally the
358 Lyn: ⌊Basic sixth grade English class
359 (Laughs)
360 Don: well I don't wanna say tha::t but
361 Lyn: ⌊Yeah but it's true.

It's clear to Lyn that Don is frustrated, and she must play a difficult role. She is both his confidante and part of the group of people who have made him so frustrated. Like Jeff, who must balance carefully his role with Erin as she vents her frustration with the "half of the class" that has not come to share her view, Lyn must talk her way through a situation that is underlaid with social, personal, and academic land mines. Even as she agrees with Don at several points that students are writing poorly and that she might be one of them, she also posits a reason why: poor teaching in high school. She offers up a new antagonist, one they can share: bad teachers who don't give students the grounding that Don feels they should and that he must now compensate for. They are both relieved of responsibility for the poor performance, and Don is positioned as a "good" teacher, one who can and unfortunately must rectify his students' flawed education. If Lyn pays for the sins of her classmates as Don reads her paper, they are both paying for the sins of the teachers who came before. Lyn will be unable to receive a thoughtful answer to her questions until Don has dealt with his feelings. But her responses ultimately seem to satisfy Don, who then goes on to discuss in more detail both the book and the movie the class is dealing with.

Don's frustration grows from caring about his students. He is angry that he can't spend the time he needs to on their papers; he is angry that he has to spend so much time on mechanical things that he knows most students don't care about when he wants to spend time on the kinds of reading and writing that excited him, that made him choose this field. He is like Rick in that "so much is going on" that he feels paralyzed, exhausted. The conference, with its surface of conversation and its underpinnings of asymmetrical power, allows him to voice his anger. From a critical perspective, what is "wrong" about this conference is not so much that Don expressed his feelings, for certainly Lyn will take away from the conference a better sense of Don as a human, as a person struggling within a web of forces and demands much like she is. But she did not have the power to withdraw from the conference; she did not have the status to insist that her topics be treated with the same respect that she treated Don's; her requests, both overt and implicit, that Don help her become a better writer, went largely ignored, and she did not have the power to contest or reshape the conference.

Because first-year writing classes are often among the smallest classes that students experience and because teachers often ask students to share personal narratives, students in those classes see the teacher as someone who knows them, someone they can approach about problems outside of class. Rick hints at having difficulty beyond Mary's class, as does Dave in his conference with Carl and Dana in her conference with Eric. And in each case, the response is the same.

239 Carl: (turn continues)   Any
240   questions or comments about that that you wanna make? That's
241   your best paper.

242 Dave: yeah (laughs) I was--
243 Carl: ⌊That's your best paper.
244 Dave: I was pleased. I wasn't expecting a grade like an A or anything
245   (little laugh).
246 Carl: It's a good paper. Hope you do that well on your next one.
247 Dave: I do too.
248 Carl: You'll be in good, well you're already in good shape, I mean
249   /you're not in any danger in class or⌈ /?/
250 Dave: ⌊/I wish it was/ just like
251   that in my other classes. (Little laugh)
252 Carl: Well, good, Dave, you take this with you.⌉
253 Dave: ⌊All right   ⌊Okay
254 Carl: And I have to do one more of these right away.
Conference Ends

What happens in our classes as we teach sometimes spills over from one class to another. When an office partner or a colleague asks us how classes are going, we may suggest a cup of coffee and try to get some good advice to improve a class going sour before we go into our next class angry and frustrated. Yet in conferences with students, when students bring up their concerns about other classes, slipping them in at the very end of the conference (how have we made room for them anywhere else?!) we may ignore those concerns, pretend the topic has not been offered, or give lip service to the problem. These problems may be spilling over into the student's performance in our classes, may be at the heart of difficulties we are otherwise at a loss to explain. If students feel insecure, afraid, unable to make the adjustment we assume they will make and let those feelings out in conferences, what does it say to them when we ignore their concerns? When we exercise our power to close down the conference, when we say goodbye, when we deal with their topic glibly? Imagine our anger and frustration if a department chair or a dean responded to fears, insecurity, concerns about teaching or tenure or the many other aspects of our lives by saying, "Thanks for sharing. It was good to talk with you. You have to go now. Goodbye." Rick insists that Mary at least *acknowledge* his affective topic, his feelings. Dave is hurried out the door. Felicia's introduction of her feelings prompted me to give her the "quick and dirty" advice she needed to make some improvement in her paper and then I dismissed her and moved on to the next student. We are not counselors, but we are speaking partners. And speaking partners do not usually ignore topics offered for discussion or dismiss them as a matter of practice.

Transforming the Personal

It is common for teachers to take a student's affective topic and transform it into a discourse topic. We resubmerge the feelings in something safe, something more clearly about writing or reading or skills and move away from feelings. In the long excerpt below from Eric and Dana's conference, Dana struggles to articulate her fears and concerns about her performance in another English class, and Eric struggles to respond. Her faith in her abilities has been shaken by this first year in college, and she needs some help in reseeing herself as a competent student. Like most students, Dana waits until near the end of the conference to discuss her feelings and ties it to a question about grades.

613 Dana: What kind of grade would you give this?
614 Eric: Oh that's a that's a good solid paper, now just let me think.
615 Dana: / ? /
616 Eric: That's probably on the line between a B and an A.
617 Dana: Okay that's good to hear. ⌈I'm glad because I was I was real
618 Eric: ⌊Yeah
619 Dana: skeptical, s- skeptical at the beginning of the semester ⌈when I
620 Eric: ⌊Yeah
621 Dana: think because my first paper I I mean, I mean, I lo- I mean I was
622   obvious after you pointed out some things that you know that,
623   know I could see why why it you recieved the grade it did but, I
624   don't, not that English has been one of my stronger p⌈oints but, it
625 Eric: ⌊Yeah
626 Dana: I mean, ⌈you know I thought it--
627 Eric: ⌊No it's a very readable pa- it's a very readable, um, uh,
628   it's a readable paper. I⌈t was no trouble reading that, it was not an
629 Dana: ⌊Kay
630 Eric: ordeal to read that paper at all. I liked reading it. ⌈Uh, and there's
631 Dana: ⌊Mkay
632 Eric: good content there. Y⌈ou know, it could be um (2 sec) the content
633 Dana: ⌊Right
634 Eric: doesn't push into the terrain of (little laugh) great insight or I
635   mean I'm not going to uh kid you but it's it's useful. ⌈It's worth
636 Dana: ⌊Mm-hmm
637 Eric: saying.

638 Dana: Okay.
639 Eric: ⌊Could be pushed a little more.

Eric addresses Dana's fear that the earlier, less successful work she had done in his class may have been more indicative of her abilities than this recent one. This piece is a strong one, and his tone is reassuring as he tells her how he felt as he read. Despite the increasing qualification of his praise as he speaks (his assessment goes from a solid B/A paper to "very readable" to "useful"), it is what Dana needs to hear. Eric establishes himself as both appreciative of Dana's abilities and honest in his response ("I'm not going to kid you"). Feeling a bit more secure, Dana continues.

640 Dana: Alright. I'm taking um 142 (a literature class) this semester, / ? /--
641 Eric: ⌊Uhkay, this
642   semester
643 Dana: ⌊Yes
644 Eric: ⌊Yeah
645 Dana: an um, I don't know, I'm not doing as well in there as I'd like,
646   I'm very borderline B C right now and um, I don't know, it's
647 Eric: ⌊Okay
648 Dana: it's just it's kinda hard for me to like pinpoint my problem and,
649   I I just I just like almost wanna ask /the guy/ /?/ can't can't
650   even think of his name now he um, his name is on the cover
651   of one of the books, the the book we use. (2 sec) The hardback
652   book.
653 Eric: ⌊A man?
654 Dana: Yeah.
655 Eric: Well, it's let's see, Robert Dean? Ian Morley?
656 Dana: Ian Morley.
657 Eric: ⌊Awright.
658 Dana: ⌊That's it. Couldn't remember his
659   name.
660 Eric: ⌊Okay.
661 Dana: An um, um, I I'm really enjoying the class I like the pieces that
662 Eric: ⌊Yes   ⌊Yes
663 Dana: we're reading, but at the sa- but it's just like, like the last um, the
664 Eric: ⌊Yeah
665 Dana: last test we had was a take home exam and um, I wrote uh a
666 Eric: ⌊Yeah
667 Dana: short essay on um, "The Yellow Wallpaper?"
668 Eric: ⌊Yeah
669 Dana: ⌊Which is a

670   story I really like I read it in high school, I love that story, and I
671 Eric: ⌊Yeah
672 Dana: thought it was--
673 Eric: ⌊And we read it.
674 Dana: Yeah, that's right.
675 Eric: ⌊Yeah
676 Dana: an um I I thought it was a fairly good paper, and then or or, a
677   a fairly good essay and then, I'm I have a real hard time with
678 Eric: ⌊Yeah
679 Dana: poems and uh, he gave me a B for my poem essay and a C for
680   my Yellow Wallpaper well I thought it would be just the
681   opposite, it's just like, I don't know, I have a real hard time
682 Eric: ⌊Yeah?   ⌊/Kay/
683 Dana: see like what it is I'm you know that I'm missing and I mean
684   it seems to be ki--
685 Eric: ⌊Have ya talked with, didja talk with Ian Morley?
686 Dana: No, I haven't talked with him.
687 Eric: ⌊He is a VERY nice guy. He is (little laugh) one of,
688   the most generous people in the entire uh de- uh department,
689   as well as one of the most intelligent, and it would be, it would
690   be worthwhile for you to go ⌈talk with the guy/ it would be
691 Dana: ⌊I think I think I should too
692 Eric: instructive. He's a fine professor.
693 Dana: I think I should. I have a tendency to be kind of, I don't, it's not
694   a very personal class, it's like five times as big as our class ⌉
695 Eric: ⌊Yeah
696 Dana: And so I'm I don't think he knows my name   ⌉
697 Eric: ⌊Yeah
698 Dana: An ⌉
699 Eric: ⌊No, I've got one of those, too. But um, he's just a very
700   generous man, and smart. I would trust the grade. ⌉
701 Dana: ⌊Mm-hmm   ⌊Yeah.
702 Eric: I I would trust that they're sensible.⌉

Dana's confusion and concerns over grading are dismissed. How can she argue with the most generous and intelligent man in the department? Instead of explaining how grades might be arrived at, instead of clearing up a mystery that is affecting Dana's sense of self as a writer and a student, Eric steps away from his colleague's class, grading, and student, although they are all connected at this moment in the conference. Dana agrees that is it a good thing to talk with your professor—after all, she is talking with one now. But she is afraid, she has no connection, the professor in question doesn't even know her name. How can she approach him? Eric offers her no advice on how to make a personal connection in such a situation, does not sympathize with her shyness, does not acknowledge her fear. Instead, he says he has such a large class, too, and returns to trusting this stranger's grading. Dana goes on to assure Eric that she does trust the grading, for it is clear that the topic of grading is not up for discussion, and attempts to better articulate her fears and concerns.

```
703  Dana:              ⌊Yeah, I I'm positive that they (the grades)
704            are (sensible), it's just um, I don't, I just, I wish there was something..
705            I don't, I /except/ I don't have a real specific question that I can
706            just go up an ask him, I just, I just wanna say, tell me what to
707            look for in the in the in the work that makes me BE insightful,
708            I mean like, like, he'll bring up things in class, and see with our
709            class I just wouldn't have thought it ⌉
710  Eric:                                         ⌊Yup
711  Dana:  And I mean I think I think it almost takes a special kind of
712            person who has a sense for those kind of things, a gift for um,
713            for knowing knowing what the author's trying to say. But I
714            mean I I've always loved to read and I guess I thought I was
715            pretty pretty good at it until (laughing) I got to college.
```

Dana is afraid to talk to this professor, whose name is on the hard cover book they are using, who is intelligent and sensible, who is so distant from her in this class where she is not doing well. What can she say? She wants to be like the successful students in this class, she wants to be like the successful student she used to be, but she has no words to approach this man with, no specific question that will allow her to get into the conversation that she wants. Just as she had to ask a specific question about her grades to get to this point in the conference, she needs such an opening to approach her other teacher. She is afraid, confused, and unsure of her abilities. Faced with so much to deal with, so much that involves feelings, Eric chooses to focus on the first part of Dana's statement in lines 711-715, which allows him to define and describe in a realm where he feels relatively safe.

```
716  Eric:  Well (5 sec, struggling to begin a word) you know the things
717            classes should do should be to sort of open you to different
718            kinds of things to look for.
719  Dana:  Mm-hmm
720  Eric:  And, I mean over the course of time (3 sec) people have the
721            experience, of sort of looking from different points of view and
```

722   also, are able somehow to synthesize a couple of those or use one
723   uh play off one point of view against another. And all of that
724   comes with time and part of the purpose of the class is I guess is
725   to sort of open up
726 Dana: Mm-hmm
727 Eric: other angles from which something can be, can be seen. So I
728   don't think it's a matter of insight or intuition, so ⌊much as
729 Dana: ⌊Mm-hmm
730 Eric: simply sort of ex experience with different sorts of contexts in
731   which a text can be taken ⌉
732 Dana: ⌊Mm-hmm ⌉
733 Eric: ⌊Up. Well--
734 Dana: ⌊For example,
735   have you read "Big Two-Hearted River."

Dana is not satisfied with Eric's response. In fact, she treats it much
like an interruption in her story of coming to feel inadequate to the
requirements of her literature class. She takes back the floor forcefully,
with none of the hesitation she has shown earlier in this conference,
interrupting Eric with "For example" as if she had never stopped
speaking. She wants him to fully understand her experience of this
class, the depth of her desire to "know" these books as her teachers do,
to regain the sense of accomplishment and prestige that she felt back
in high school. She does not want a distanced, conceptual explanation
of learning; she wants a personal response to a personal problem.

736 Eric: No, I've never read that.⌉
737 Dana: ⌊Mkay
738 Eric: ⌊Sorry.
739 Dana: Alright, tryin to think of another story. It was a fairly long um
740   story, and what I got out of it was that it was a man who went on
741   a fishing trip. I mean that that's what I got out of it (laughing).
742 Eric: ⌊Mm-hmm
743 Dana: An then we discussed it in class yesterday and he brought up
744   all these points and um, and it wasn't just him bringing up the
745   points there were other students ⌊in the class who who you know
746 Eric: ⌊Yeah
747 Dana: found something out, you know, that it was, you know, he it
748   going fishing, he was getting away from past worries, an an um,
749   I don't know, I'm sitting there like dumbfounded, like how did
750   you know that, you know what I'm saying? An um, I mean it
751 Eric: ⌊Mm-hmm

752 Dana: it was really, I mean after that the story seemed much more in
753   depth than I thought it was and I could s- it was an interesting
754 Eric: Mm-hmm, mm-hmm
755 Dana: story and I'd like to read it again. You know whereas the first
756 Eric: Mm-hmm
757 Dana: time I read it I thought that it was a long story about a fishing trip.
758   And so--
759 Eric: Well, I mean one (laughs), one sort one sort of way to
760   go, is to, is to, pick out any two items in a text, and ask what they
761   have to do with each other. No, um, uh (laughs) whatever the
762 Dana: Mm-hmm
763 Eric: answer it's gonna be interesting. I mean if you if you can show
764   that they're redundant, that if the sense is the second one is the
765   first one over again in some way, you will be moving towards
766   the author's meaning, the author's intention, because we
767 Dana: Mm-hmm
768 Eric: communicate meaning by redundancy, that is by saying the same
769   things in different ways.
770 Dana: Mkay.
771 Eric: Okay. If you CAN'T explain what the two have, what
772   the two have to do with each other, then I mean there are two
773   possiblities. One is you yet haven't spotted the nature of the
774   redundancy, or secondly there really is a break in the text. And
775   there's a sense in which these two things don't have anything to
776   do with each other, and so the question then arises how to
777   explain that. That is, how to explain the break in the
778 Dana: Mm-hmm
779 Eric: text.
780 Dana: Mm-hmm
781 Eric: Okay. / ? / So I mean one way to go, well you say it's a long
782   story about fishing. (Laughing) A long story about fishing.
783   Well, you know, I what I say is, having any two details at any
784   distance from each other in the text, you can sort of interrogate
785   with respect to what they have to do with each other. And what
786 Dana: Mm-hmm
787 Eric: a- whatever answer you come up with (2 sec) either you're able
788   to say what they have to do with each other or you can't say,
789   you're going to be off and running on a kind of
790   investigation.
791 Dana: Mm-hmm. Mkay. Alright.
792 Eric: Yeah, so when you talk about in depth, of something in depth,
793   basically what you're talking about I mean people are either
794   able to show an author's meaning as redundantly substantiated

795   in the text on the one hand, or else, are going to be dealing with
796 Dana: Mm-hmm
797 Eric: sort of ruptures in the text, and attempting to account for
798   that / ? / various kinds of explanation ⌉
799 Dana: ⌊Mm-hmm
800 Eric: / ? / one's interesting.
801 Dana: That's, those are good, um points. I mean I think I can use that
802   like in the rest of stories we read, I mean I can try to, I don't
803   know, look for, cause I mean there were things in the story that I
804   thought of um, since you haven't read the story you know I
805   don't wanna go into it, but I mean, there were things I kinda
806   questioned when I was kinda like, what is the author tryin to
807   say, that in fact were the things that people brought up, but it
808   was just like I didn't see what those things were supposed to say,
809   I just questioned them, whereas others in the class could be like,
810   hey, wuh well I think this means this. You know what I⌉m--
811 Eric: ⌊Well
812   uh right, I I mean uh the proof for that, that this means this, has
813   always got to be, I mean, the showing of some sort ⌠of
814 Dana: ⌊Right
815 Eric: redundancy, how B is A over again in some convincing
816   way.⌉
817 Dana: ⌊Mm-hmm. Okay. Awright.
818 Eric: Other than that I mean there would be much, it would be, uh,
819   it's a very arbitrary matter, I mean this represents the /pea/ that
820   symbol⌠zes order, well how do you know?
821 Dana: ⌊Mm-hmm   Right.
822 Eric: I mean it's like, what the color green a symbol for, well
823   anything you like, jealousy, hope and so on. I mean the the the
824   uh the test is, redundancy within the text.
825 Dana: Uh-huh
826 Eric: But then there's also the fact of the matter that texts are not
827   perfectly redundant, there are breaks that sort of open the text to
828   the rest of the world.
829 Dana: Ri:ght.
830 Eric: You know. Okay Dana, I'll se⌠e you then tomorrow.⌉
831 Dana: ⌊Awright.   ⌊Okay
832   Thank you for your time.
833 Eric: Okay. See you later.
Conference Ends.

Eric offers Dana a strategy for "being insightful," but it's not clear
that Dana understands how meaning is "redundantly substantiated

within a text." She recognizes what he is trying to do, however, and thanks him for the advice. But her thanks and her small attempt to explain how she might use this strategy give way again to the narrative that she has been trying to tell Eric. This is the ending that gives her a bit of hope, perhaps prompted in part by Eric's apparent confidence in her ability not just to read and interpret literature but to understand his discussion of redundancy and ruptures in the text. By the end of her story, she is seeing and questioning aspects of the written text, even if she doesn't know how to create meaning like others in her class. She has been dumbfounded, shown up by her classmates who seem to have some special gift or knowledge, but she senses that if she can understand Eric's advice, she might be one of the insightful ones in her course, might regain that sense of personal skill and ability that she has lost.

Dana seems, at the end, stunned into minimal responses by the strategy thrown at her; she has told her story and received an academic response. But at least it took time, the professor took time; for students, this simple aspect of a conference—that a teacher takes the time to talk with them—is almost enough to mitigate any disappointments or failures that might have occurred in that conference. Eric has addressed her fears only obliquely, has responded to her story with a lecture, has avoided the personal and emotional. He has failed to personally respond to Dana's emotions, transforming them instead into a matter of learning a skill. He has ignored any discussion of the economy of the classroom, where participation and knowledge of a particular kind can buy you a spot up front after class, talking in more detail with the professor who will then know your name and mark you as "insightful." And it is likely that Dana will fail in her attempt to use the strategy Eric offered in place of exploring her concerns; she can try to use it, she says with uncertainty, but she still doesn't know exactly what to look for. Her uncertainty about her ability to use Eric's advice leads her back to the fear, uncertainty, and frustration she felt in the classroom. What college teachers want and whether she can meet those expectations has been the emotional topic that has bracketed this entire conference but has not been the clear topic of discussion at any point throughout. Despite Eric's understanding that meaning is made from redundancy, he has not apparently noticed the repetition of Dana's topics: fear of failure, loss of self-confidence, frustration in learning. This final part of the conference, so important to Dana's sense of herself as a student, has been wasted.

Responding to Feelings

Learning is not always a rational, logical process. It is experiential, emotional, and messy. I didn't wake up one morning and say, "I think I'll become a feminist now. And I think I'll combine that with critical sociolinguistics." A series of experiences and emotional responses to those experiences shaped my perceptions, my desires, my curiousity, my needs. I found feminism and a critical approach to language and power attractive (not necessarily right or logical). I found reading books and talking about them to be fun, exciting, challenging and satisfying in ways that mathematics wasn't. I loved the way words could be shaped, the way I could write what I couldn't say, the time and space that writing offered me, and the acceptance and praise that came with success in that area. Our students are involved in that same search, that same process of shaping and being shaped, of choosing and being drawn toward ways of knowing, learning, making sense of their worlds.

I'd like to return to this chapter's epigraph by Pamela Fishman. As we decide what will be talked about in these conferences—and it appears that it is, overwhelmingly, teachers who make that decision—we are choosing to orient ourselves to ideas, to skills, to texts but not to emotions, to humans. To be honest with you, I have not been in enough other teachers' classrooms to say whether this is a disjunctive behavior or a continuation of the classroom. I know that many of my colleages search for topics and activities that students "like," issues that really "get them going," that get them "excited," that raise the emotional pitch of the classroom and involve students in discussion that counts to them. They want to connect their assignments to students' lives in important ways. Yet, aside from early semester "get to know you" conferences, the rest of the conferences are focused on texts, on improving skills with the written word, on raising poor grades by revising earlier texts. We set aside the joy of writing, the urgency of communicating with others, the anger or sorrow or fear or connection that generates writing in favor of a dispassionate examination of errors, lapses in logical thinking, and problems with textual focus. For as much as we may "feel" that conferences are about emotion as well as fact and convention, institutionally we are judged not on how good our students feel about writing but on how well they have mastered the conventions of writing for an academic audience, sometimes on discrete skills that can be tested quantitatively.

Many teachers schedule an initial conference during which they ask a number of questions about the student's experiences, goals, concerns, and background. I have done the same, and afterward, like many of my colleagues, have felt that since I now "know" the student and she has had a chance to talk about her feelings and get them all out, I can go on to focus intensely on writing for the rest of the semester. It's as if I was talking to myself, head buried in my student's text; it's so odd now to realize that I believed she would have no more new feelings or no resurgence of old ones over the semester, or even that I had "dealt" with all her concerns in a first conference.

I believe many students have difficulty finding ways to disrupt the teacher's narrative, the teacher's control of topics in order to introduce their own affective topics because they do not know either how to connect them to the teacher's topics or they cannot transform the discourse topic into an affective one in the same way teachers transform their students' topics. Teachers are usually polished speakers in many registers, but many students, while polished speakers with peers, have had little experience speaking in extended turns in a classroom or in significantly reshaping academic discourse. Further, when speakers of different status are involved in talk, the speaker of higher status and power usually has control over topic acknowledgment and development; he or she can choose to ignore or take up the partner's speech while the speaker of lesser power usually must acknowledge or take up the topics offered by the more powerful speaker. (Incidences where this does not occur provide the basis for humor or tragedy, particularly in British comedy or drama, where class and status differences are so readily acknowledged.)

Making Space

So what can students ask about that will help them get the floor with an affective topic? Grades. It is not only an almost set-in-stone requirement that teachers respond to questions about grading, but it is also a permissible moment for students to express emotion about the grade. That emotional expression may also open the floor for an explanation, which may in turn open up the space needed for a narrative and the offering of other affective topics. So we hear Dana explaining that she was worried about the grade and pleased with what she received, *because*— and here she can tell Eric the story of how she used to perform and how concerned she is now because of her other class, and so on. Grading is both specific—students can ask particularized questions—and subjective, open to debate. Furthermore, for most first-year students, grades are correlated with feelings: if they really liked the topic or felt good while writing the piece, then they believe it should receive a good grade. The text is not as important as the feelings. So a discussion of grades opens the floor for students to begin talking about a host of other concerns and feelings.

In the conferences I've observed, listened to tapes of, and done myself, the pattern is for the teacher not to bring up the topic of grades until the end of the conference or not to bring it up at all. If the teacher does not bring up grades and instead asks simply if there are any more questions, students are likely at that point to ask about grades. They may ask what grade they received, they may ask whether following the teacher's advice will improve the grade, or they may say that they aren't happy with the grade or some other variation. In any case, they have set up the structure needed to include a justification for the question or comment, and have gained the floor. But it is often too late. Most conferences cannot go on indefinitely, and once the teacher has asked whether the student has any questions, has completed her agenda, other topics raised may be given short shrift as the teacher worries about fitting in the next student and the one after that. Student topics appear to be less important, peripheral to whatever goal the teacher has wanted to achieve. And so those students who do not insist on their topics being taken seriously by reintroducing them after they have been dismissed find themselves, like Dave and Mike, being allowed a scant few turns of speech before being turned out the door. Rick, Dana, and John all repeatedly offer their topics until they are dealt with in more depth, and they do so through a larger portion of the conference. But they must work hard at disrupting the teacher's march onward through the preset agenda, and the response is slender.

One way to encourage students to speak more freely about their feelings is to consider those affective topics as valid and to address them squarely. There are two problems with this: sometimes we don't recognize a topic as affective, for it is bundled up in the clothing of discourse topics and we are focused on talking about writing and not feelings about writing. A second difficulty is that conferences are usually limited to a short period of time. If we have

recognized a topic as affective, then often we find ourselves deciding whether the time we have left will allow us to fit in discussion
of both the student topic (and the topics it may lead to) and the
topics we had preset in our heads as we began the conference. But
often, if we do not address those emotions, all the advice we offer
may not be heard or will be heard through the frame of those
unaddressed concerns. It is a question of time, but it may be a
more valuable use of time for both teacher and student to address
their concerns in more than one conference.

Although I have made frequent use of student and teacher agendas created shortly in advance of conferences, it's also been my experience that students don't write down that they are angry or
frustrated or scared and want to talk about that. They will write
down that they want to talk about getting better grades or want to
discuss the grade on paper number two or to get some strategies for
revising that will help ALL their work. That usually signals me that
my agenda should be short and flexible. Providing enough time
when it is needed has meant for me that later conferences are more
focused, more comfortable, and—judging from student response
and textual changes—more successful.

Obviously, a simple strategy is to make space for affective topics
earlier in the conference and more clearly before we have firmly set
the conference shape in our heads. If students need to have a specific
question to help them take the floor, we might ask them about their
grading concerns earlier in the conference, or open the conference up
to talk about their other classes. But questions and answers are usually syntagmatic; that is, a question compels an answer, especially
when there is a difference in power and status between asker and
answerer. So it is difficult for students to not answer the questions
asked of them. Bill, for example, asks Cari early on in the conference
what she "likes best" about her paper. But he doesn't follow up on it,
moving instead to another question, which she must then answer
instead of developing her first response.

When students submit personal papers, teachers often ask them
about some of the incidents they describe. Students write sometimes
to meet two needs, producing something personally important to
them and then realizing that they must submit it to the scrutiny and
critique of a teacher, much like the conference I described with my
poetry professor. But it's important not to abuse the power we have
to force students to respond when they do not wish to, instead asking

students questions that might allow them to move to whatever ground they are more comfortable on: "What would you change about this if you revised it? Why?" "Which sections worked particularly well for you?" And certainly we can offer our emotional responses to the writing; we are not dispassionate readers who find a piece "useful" to read. Often, doing so encourages students to share their own emotional responses to their writing, and they begin to speak of other concerns or feelings that have helped or hindered them in their course work—the kinds of feelings and history that also keep conferences from working successfully.

It is important also to remember that gender plays a role in the emotional aspects of conferencing. In the study conferences, female students brought up many more affective topics than male students, though they were roughly equal in offering discourse topics. In their written accounts of conferencing, female students emphasize the importance of acknowledging feelings in a conference. How well their feelings are attended to has an important effect on the outcome of a conference: "Some profs will act like your (sic) bothering them. They act very anxious, which makes you feel yucky so you leave just as lost as you were before." It doesn't matter if what the teacher said might have been helpful; because the student feels uncomfortable, no learning takes place.

Male students, of course, also mention feelings. It was a male student who commented on how important it was to him that his teacher asked him about his hometown and his sports involvement. Nonetheless, the feelings males indicate are often quite different from what female students reveal. Male students are angry when the conferences do not live up to their expectations; female students are discouraged and even more uncertain about their abilities. Male students are likely to see unsuccessful conferences as a violation of their right to know whatever it is the teacher knows that will be helpful to them; female students are more likely to see unsuccessful conferences as a lost opportunity to establish a better relationship.

These differences are consistent with important findings by researchers in women's cognitive development, such as Mary Belenkey, et al. (1986), Carol Gilligan (1982), and Nancy Chodorow (1978). In response to ethical dilemmas, males, these researchers argue, focus on the abstract concept of justice, applied equally to each individual. Women focus on the relationship of individuals to a larger system and to each other. They conclude that males are more concerned with autonomy, females with community. These differing orientations affect more than ethical decision-making. Black, et al. (1994) found that when young writers submitted portfolios of work to anonymous readers, males positioned the readers as judges of individual work and saw the portfolio as a chance to "showcase" or present skills. Female writers, however, saw the portfolio as an extension of the self and positioned evaluators as trusted readers who had the power to hurt the writer through insensitivity to feelings. Understanding these possible gender differences may help teachers deal with the affective dimensions of conferencing, may help them understand student reactions and needs, even help understand their own needs and reactions. The emotional responses all participants experience may well be connected to gender.

I have been writing here about talking with students one-to-one about feelings. But it may not be just one student who is feeling frustrated or scared or even excited about writing or the course or their other coursework. A great deal can be addressed in class itself. I used to feel that I had to provide all the answers for all the problems; now I feel that I have to create an atmosphere where problems can be articulated and as a group we can offer solutions or changes. In first-year classes where many students are shocked by their poor performance by mid-semester, I have set aside class time for students to work in groups of their choice to voice their concerns and problems then share those as they feel comfortable. Students work in groups or as a whole class to offer solutions. In some cases, we have changed the structure of my course to provide more feedback or to examine (in the absence of a college-wide writing across the curriculum program) writing from various fields so that students could understand the difficulties they were experiencing in adapting to different contexts and demands. We spent more time looking at sample papers and talking about how they would be graded; I did a "spoken protocol" to show how I responded as I read and how I re-read and graded. I have opened departmental grading sessions (at least the training/calibration sessions preceding them) to students who return to share what they learned with classmates. And students who have personal problems—roommates, family, boyfriend/girlfriend, fraternity/sorority obligations or decisions—have often found advice from classmates or been urged to speak with particular people or support services. Dialogue journals read and responded to by classmates have provided a place to vent (for me as well!) and get responses ranging from sympathy to clear-headed advice. In upper level classes, we deal with concerns about life after college, with job searches and graduate school, and tie writing and talk to those concerns. I am sometimes an observer, sometimes an active participant in these discussions. But it has always been apparent to me that in a goal-based class such as mine, spending class time in this way is crucial if we are to reach our goals; it is time spent identifying road blocks and charting new directions. We have a shared knowledge base and a place to begin that opens up conferences to talk about feelings, that ties conferences to classes in ways that are important and personal, not simply institutional. And it means that in conferences later, when a student says "you know," I really do.

CHAPTER SIX

Possibilities

I SETTLED BACK IN THE BIG GREEN CHAIR AND READ THE TRANSCRIBED words of students and teachers. I read my own words in journals and old transcripts. I looked at data sheets and columns of numbers. Then I asked myself a question that surprised me, that was deceptively simple: What do I want to happen as a result of my conferencing?

I realized that I had hoped when I began to research conferencing that I would find real change was taking place, that I would learn how to conference with more skill and compassion. That I would learn how to challenge—even in small ways—the same structures that made me feel so inadequate as a student, that kept me convinced for so long that failure and success was always and completely an individual matter, that made me feel—even briefly—ashamed of my family, myself, and my knowledge. I lost that hope initially, momentarily overwhelmed by the repetitive control, conference after conference, that helps socialize students (and reaffirm teachers) into patterns that make possible the kind of anger and humiliation I described in the introduction. But over the course of this work, I recast the questions I began with. Where I had started by asking "What's going on in conferencing?" I ended up asking, "What *could* happen in conferencing?"

What could happen between a teacher and a student that would move us toward a better world? I thought again of bell hooks's goal to educate for freedom. I went from "realist" to "idealist" because for me, that is the only movement that makes sense. And, where I once saw a conference as a clearly bounded event, a static "thing" much like a box which contains other, more active things, I now see conferences as dynamic and permeable, interwoven—sometimes closely, sometimes distantly—with many other aspects of our lives. I began to ask myself questions that I could answer, should answer: Why do I conference? Are conferences an extension of my classroom practice? Are they a repair for what goes on in my classroom? Are they a repair for what I see going on outside my classroom? What do I challenge? What do I affirm? Do my students know what I am doing in and with my conferences? What do my students think about all this stuff?

The questions I consider in this final chapter are concerned with practice and ideology, goals and people. I feel powerful enough to believe that I can make something happen; I recognize my privileged position and need to understand more clearly how I intend to use that position. I need to consider not just how the students sitting in the classroom will be affected by what I do and will themselves affect me, but how these conferences that slide by one after another support or challenge or change a much larger system of power, access, and learning. Over the course of this chapter, I will examine the connection between critical discourse analysis and critical pedagogy and consider how the goals of critical pedagogy might lead us toward "third-generation" conferencing. Student descriptions of conferencing help me bridge the gap between what we hope for and what seems to happen. I will include some suggestions for conferencing that grow out of consideration of the research conferences, my own conferencing, and the goals of a critical classroom. It was my own sense of frustration and failure in conferencing that prompted me to begin this research, and I want to end it—temporarily at least—with the kinds of questions and possibilities that I see for my future conferencing practice. It's like any fishing story—there's always hope, there's always another chance.

Critical Discourse Analysis and Critical Pedagogy

In *Life in Schools* (1989), Peter McLaren provides us with a look at the devastating ways in which social class, education, and gender are all intertwined in an urban school. He argues that

> We claim to live in a meritocracy where social salvation is supposedly achieved through scholastic merit: every student will, more or less, reap the academic awards of his or her own initiative, regardless of sex, religion, or family background. That all sounds fine on the surface, but in reality it's simply hollow rhetoric ... I believe ... it's the latent function of

the educational system to maintain the status quo, including existing social inequities. (151)

He asks us to be reflective teachers, to examine our own practices and ask questions about the ways in which knowledge is constructed in our classrooms. We should consider, for example, the kinds of speech we value, the kinds of experience we privilege, and the ways in which our students not only resist being drawn into the dominant ideology of our culture but the ways in which we resist being drawn into *their* lives, experiences, and language. McLaren comes to realize that he has not been appreciating all that his impoverished students bring to the classroom. Rather, he has been pitying them, and in his liberal pity, he has attempted to instill in them his middle-class white values, assuming without question that these values are "better." He has attempted to reproduce himself and the system he now sees has helped construct the situation which limits these children's access to learning and controls their lives.

I keep returning to the classroom—I must, for it is really where conferences begin. If we want students to be active learners and teachers in conferences, they must also occupy such roles in the class-room. Ideally, a conference should be an extension of the classroom. By that I mean that conferences shouldn't be scheduled because a teacher must repair the dynamics of the classroom, nor does it make sense to see learning as discrete, bounded events—the result of this lesson plan and that conference. Just as a teacher considers goals (her own and her students) for the class and how they will be worked toward or achieved, she needs as well to consider the role that confer-encing will play in achieving those goals. For teachers practicing crit-ical pedagogy, McLaren outlines connections between knowledge and power and how they might be considered in the classroom.

> Knowledge is relevant only when it begins with the experiences students bring with them from the surrounding culture; it is critical only when those experiences are shown to sometimes be problematic (i.e. racist, sex-ist); and it is transformative only when students begin to use the knowl-edge to help empower others. Knowledge then becomes linked to social reform. (189-190)

Conferencing has been posited by a large number of composition-ists as a way to enter our students' lives, to get to know them better, to listen to them speak (or to allow them to speak) outside the rigid framework of most classrooms. (Note the assumption that classroom structure cannot be fundamentally changed, only offset by outside activities.) It was to be a way to validate student experiences and language, a meeting place where teachers and students could be "just people," could be identified less by their institutional roles and more by their beliefs and experiences. The need to learn about our students acknowledges the increasing diversity of classrooms and the gap between the middle-class values of teachers and the values of their students. However, the effort to get to know our students is not entirely innocent. It is usually the means to an end—to find effective ways to bring them into the fold. In the context of the classroom as a neutral site where "facts" and common-sense knowledge about what is right and good are dispensed (and although this notion has taken a beating in academe, I would argue that it is a belief still widely held outside the academy), conferencing is presented as humane, compassionate, a personalized way to help those who have not seen the rightness or understood the facts. Even in liberal classrooms, where difference may not be ignored or repressed but is "celebrated" in thematic units on diversity, conferences still function to find ways to subordinate the personal experience and language of students to a dominant world view—the teacher's. Many of the teachers who taped their conferences with me consider themselves to be feminists, Marxists, people of strong social conscience sharing the common goal of changing what they see as systemic inequality in our culture. In their curricula, they introduce students to materials that critique the educational system, the class system, and the race and gender constructions that permeate our culture. I admire and respect their beliefs. But there is a disturbing disjunction between their goals and their practice.

Bell hooks argues that many teachers are unable to critically consider their pedagogy because they are afraid; they have so identified themselves as a teacher that they cannot question that identity. As teachers (and students), we have become used to the difference in power, in status, that our institutional positions offer us. Some of us, privileged by our race or class and surrounded by others of the same race or class and values, have become used to that particular kind of power as well. This is why for so many teachers, students, and parents, a shift to critical pedagogy—the sharing of power, the shifting of some responsibilities, the change in speech and learning patterns, the suddenly released voices of those we have silenced—feels "wrong," is difficult for us, sometimes in ways we cannot clearly articulate. We are not used to this sudden "conversation" in the class-room. Others are afraid to change their practice because students often resist empowering pedagogies—they have been conditioned to believe that the teacher has all the answers and will give them to students. And when they resist pedagogy they resist teachers. "I found that there was much more tension in the diverse classroom setting where the philosophy of teaching is rooted in critical pedagogy and (in my case) feminist critical pedagogy. The presence of tension—and at times even conflict—often meant that my students did not enjoy my classes or love me, their professor, as I secretly wanted them to do" (hooks, 41-42). And when teachers are faced with poor evalua-tions, they use whatever practice has served them better; the eco-nomics of their job and the institution force them back into old patterns. In a dialog, Ron Scapp and bell hooks point out that teach-ers will often change their curriculum and include new texts, but will not alter their pedagogy substantially. They can control those texts, present them and the messages they could potentially send exactly as they have presented canonical texts. But as hooks puts it, "Education as the practice of freedom is not just about liberatory knowledge, it's about liberatory practice" (147).

What happens in many classrooms, then, is a kind of surface respect, a civil distance and a friendly control. Henry Giroux (1988) describes the "pedagogy of cordial relations" as a particularly insidi-ous form of teaching.

> Defined as the "other," students now become objects of inquiry in the interest of being understood so as to be more easily controlled. The knowledge, for example, used by teachers with these students is often drawn from cultural forms identified by class, race, and gender specific interests. But relevance, in this instance, has little to do with emancipa-tory concerns; instead, it translates into pedagogical practices that attempt to appropriate forms of student and popular culture in the inter-ests of maintaining social control. (127)

When I read this description, I asked myself: "Why do I ask my students to tell me about themselves? What kinds of information do I want to know? Toward what end will I use that information? What do I tell them in return? What don't I tell them? How is my asking for this information—a teacher asking a student—different from me asking a colleague? How does power work in this situation?" I had no answer I was proud of.

Critical discourse analysis is in many ways a counterpart to critical pedagogy. Peter McLaren argues that critical pedagogues are "united in their objectives: to empower the powerless and transform existing social inequities and injustices" (160). Like critical discourse analysts, critical educators are not merely interested in describing the ways in which power and knowledge are welded—and wielded—but are crucially concerned with examining abuse of power, the ethics of knowledge and teaching, and the effects upon human beings. It is to teach and analyze from a position that is at once profoundly theoretical and profoundly personal. If the kinds of critical discourse analysis that has informed the research in this book is capable of interrogating the contexts of language and the construction of knowledge and power with a goal of transforming systemic inequality, then critical pedagogy appears to be the approach most likely to achieve that goal. The analysis of language, of the transcripts we've read here, is part of that reflective and critical practice that McLaren and others call for.

Conferencing offers enormous potential for reproducing individually the inequities of the classroom and culture. Students have told me repeatedly that one reason conferences are so meaningful is that it's only in a conference that a student hears what's really important. They've explained that in a classroom, the teacher has to talk to everybody, has to "water down" information because it's spread across a wide range of skills and backgrounds. They assert that in a conference, however, you find out "what really counts." One student wrote to me that "if a teacher says something important in class, she really could mean it's important to the guy across the room. But if you hear it in a conference, then you know it's important, because it's directed to you."

What this student is saying, in one way, is that education that counts (counts toward what?!) is not generally occurring in the classroom, where differences between students are not acknowledged and the discourse is one of homogeneity. What the conferences I've studied show, however, is that the "personalization" of conferences consists largely of overtly dealing with the ways in which each individual student has not met expectations of punctuation, support, organization, and adherence to a correct point of view, and unconsciously affirming or addressing breaches of socially constructed roles: student-teacher, male-female. Thus Erin openly instructs Jeff on how deep-thinking students would approach a particular issue; she also instructs him—by insisting on her right to speak—that the teacher-student relationship overrides the conventional female-male dynamic from which Jeff operates. Likewise, Cari is affirmed in her observation of traditional female-male, student-teacher relationships, receiving praise and information as a result of her conventional performance. Giroux argues that "language is inseparable from lived experience" (116). We see Cari drawing on her experiences as a female and a student, reenacting that experience again in her pattern of discourse. We see teachers, experienced in power, using language powerfully to recreate that power constantly.

Critical reflection means asking ourselves as teachers questions about what seems to be ordinary and natural. Although the instructors in these conferences ask their students why they chose a particular syntactic construction or why they believe a particular reading of a text is right, they do not ask themselves the same questions. Even as Eric is critiquing rules about the use of *and*, he is replacing them with another rule. Even as he is explaining the value of working from our own experience of the text, he is demanding that Dana see her paper as an argument. (Are all our experiences arguments?) Proof rests on redundancy, he insists, and yet the proof of our lives rests on various and singular experiences, as well as redundancy. He argues that the papers we write are not fictions. And yet, I can remember papers I've written that *were* fictions, that were constructions of "truth" given to me by a teacher, unexplained and unjustified, disconnected from my own experience of the text. If I didn't give him back his "truth" in my paper, I would fail. His truth was my fiction. So I wrote fiction.

The authoritative discourse of the instructors in these conferences leaves little space for student voices or stories, even halting, tentative, brief ones. John, for example, attempts to tell the story of his own unsuccessful experiences with peer critiques, and Nina responds by asserting that she already knows what John knows. By doing so, she has closed up the little space John had created for teaching *her*. John also calls into question one of the fundamental assumptions of most writing teachers—that they can improve students' writing through their commentary on it. John argues that he does everything that Nina suggests he do and still, the paper doesn't turn out as he wishes it to. Actually, his complaint may be double-edged. Perhaps he wishes the paper to turn out as Nina does, in which case, Nina's comments are not helpful in achieving that goal.

Or perhaps he is emphasizing the difference between what he thinks is good and what Nina does. Nina's response is a defense of her practice, her ability to provide helpful comments; she suggests that John is unrealistic in expecting good writing to happen quickly (although in many ways our usual commentary suggests that improvement *will* be significant and swift).

What Nina has done in these two instances is to silence John's complaints and questions, an act that is repeated again and again in these conferences. Rather than opening up the space to create a dialogue where teacher and student can interrogate each other's beliefs and practices, a space which provides the distance needed for critical reflection, the authority of the teacher is invoked and acted on without question by the teacher, though with some resistance from students. And sometimes students desire that authority when we would rather not comply. We need critical reflection just as much at such times.

When teachers do leave open those spaces tentatively created by students, then the traditional hierarchies of knowledge and power shift. In chapter one, I provided part of a transcript from Mary and Rick's conference, during which Rick told an extended story about his grandfather's death. For some period of time, Mary ignores opportunities to shift the talk back to a teaching register. Instead, she helps to support its construction, asking him to clarify details now and then. For more than one hundred lines, Rick controls the talk of the conference, occupying a powerful position not ordinarily available to students. Giroux notes that school is a site where stories can be told and where personal and historical connections can be made as students explore their experiences in a new web of social relationships; stories beget stories, invite comparison and analysis. Extended narratives like Rick's are uncommon; the teachers on these tapes are reluctant to acquiesce to the demands of storytelling. But even short narratives can briefly shift power relations. Remember Dana's story about her difficulty in her literature class? Eric eventually takes back the floor, but Dana forces Eric to listen to her, even for a short period of time. Jeff, too, attempts to tell the story about how he wrote the draft Erin is responding to. But he places his story at the very beginning of the conference, and since there is no context to help Erin make sense of it, she interrupts to take control and read the new draft on her own terms. Stories, apparently, must be well-placed to provide students the opportunity to speak at length. But when they are, they provide a significant challenge to the control usually exercised by instructors.

Stories by teachers can be crucial as well. Michele Grijalva began to transform the resistance she encountered with her native American students by telling a story about her own experiences as a child in a native American culture. Victor Villanueva speaks openly about his continuing struggle with writing, the ways in which his home language and ways of thinking clash with the conventions of academic discourse. "I speak of such things in the courses I teach not only for the sake of those from Latino backgrounds, but for all. There can be no telling of the linguistic backgrounds of the students" (88). In my classes, I speak of my own frustrations in college, of the struggle to speak and write in acceptable ways, and I speak with love and joy about my family and the ways we speak with one another.

Through our stories, through our power, we must be "facilitators" (hooks, 156). In almost every conference I've ever listened to, the relationship between the participants is set at the very beginning by the teacher. Typically, the instructor will ask the student what he or she had brought that day, as if the student is bringing gifts to a royal personage. Or the instructor will "allow" the student to set the agenda, asking what the student wants to talk about, what questions they have about the text. In those instances, the questions become the gift, allowing the teacher to talk from that point onward, usually dealing with the student's question quickly and moving on to the teacher's agenda. I know these patterns very well because they are the two I have consistently used in past conferences. In the classroom and in the conference, we must use our power to "authorize" speech to forward student goals, to teach for critical knowledge. That means that any agenda we set must be flexible, for as parties learn they change their minds, their goals, their beliefs and values.

In chapter one, I outlined the differences between conversation and teacher-talk; they are significant particularly in terms of control and negotiation of meaning. In conversation, topics are developed and supported mutually. Speakers self-select, and shape in negotiated. That kind of structure is even more rare in these conferences than narratives—I find it only between Don and Lyn.

In the first half of the conference, Don is in control, and the conference moves roughly along. The excerpt below begins when Lyn shifts the conference to a conversation about the current class text, *A Clockwork Orange*, catching Don by surprise.

402 Don: But I think uh aside from that I think that
403   you know the ideas you've got n that you you've argued in
404   that papers are good, n I think know. (2 sec) Generally you
405   make a lot of sense I mean in arguing for Alex's uh (4 sec)
406   Alex's.. necessity of choice.
407 Lyn: (6 sec) That was a pretty good book.
408 Don: Huh?
409 Lyn: It was a pretty good book.
410 Don: (3 sec) Yeah. Dya like the book or the movie better.
411 Lyn: (2 sec) See I dunno they both had their strengths I think um
412   (4 sec) I dunn actually it'd probably be a toss-up. I don't mind
413   either way. (2 sec) There's parts that were in the book that
414   weren't in the movie an..there's visualizations in the movie
415   that you didn't see in the book. ⌐
416 Don: ⌊Basil the snake isn't in the
417   book. ⌐
418 Lyn: ⌊Mm-hmm
419 Don: (2 sec) Um..In the movie he never sees ┌he--
420 Lyn: ⌊What about when pulls
421   the drawer out with the watches n everything that's not in the
422   book.
423 Don: No.
424 Lyn: But that was a good touch. ⌐
425 Don: ⌊Oh┌yeah.
426 Lyn: ⌊I liked that.
427 Don: He nev the he never sees th the name of the book...with F-
428 Lyn: ⌊Yeah, I
429 Don: ┌Alexander is writing um--   Cause I thought it, uh
430 Lyn: ⌊didn't like that. I didn't like that.
431 Don: because I thought it
432 Lyn: (2 sec) I thought it takes like from the core a the book.
433 Don: Yeah I ┌think it does too.
434 Lyn: ⌊I mean that just strikes you ┌with that
435 Don: ⌊I mean it just it you know he's
436   his then his attack into F Alexander's home just becomes a lot
437   mindless violence.
438 Lyn: /Yes/ exactly an it's not like..he doesn't seems to connect
439   anything.
440 Don: Yeah. I mean F Alexander becomes just sort of another victim
441   for him rather uh having any kind of special meaning.
442 Lyn: Mm-hmm
443 Don: You know he comes back in the end an he has special meaning
444   because he you know it's he returns to the place but um

445 Lyn: He doesn't seem to foreshadow anything.
446 Don: No...No an I think that's where the movie loses out. I th the
447   more I read it the more I like th book and uh..probably because
448   the movie I think ends after it does after that twentieth chapter
449   / ?/...Uh I dunn I'm ambiv- very ambivalent about Alex
450   because I like h- I like what he does I don't like his /stuff/ but I
451   really just think his..control of the language and of uh his
452   control of the whole story is is fantastic.
453 Lyn: Well it is--
454 Don: ⌊You know. But he's he's a /little bigot/ he's a rotten little
455   s.o.b. I think (Lyn laughs). Well I mean you know it's nobody's
456   gonna cheer for Alex I mean. Although we end up cheering for
457   him. We end up laughing about him.
458 Lyn: ⌊I did.
459 Don: Well why is that?
460 Lyn: You have to respect him for the /scum/ that he is... You know?
461   I dunn I just he has character. Seems like you could find part of
462   him in you.. I mean he wanted to go /onto this thing/ to get
463   better but, he didn't wanna get better he wanted /out/.
464 Don: Yeah.
465 Lyn: ⌊An I can understand that n you're like well I've probably done
466   that a million times with things.
467 Don: Yeah I mean we all look for the path of least resistance you know
468   the easy way out. Um yeah Alex has there's a certain know
469   Alex (2 sec) for whatever di uh destruction an an violent and I
470   guess negative qualities he has there's uh uh mean he takes a
471   real--
472 Lyn: ⌊/???/ (simultaneous conference in the office is quite loud)
473 Don: He takes a real joy in what he does I mean really um (4 sec) You
474   know I mean you know that whatever thy thy hand shall do
475   God do so with all thy strength. Alex does that and it uh you
476   know I mean it's... We would look an say you know he's doin the
477   wrong thing but.. He does it with all of his strength and there's
478   something know he has a great force of will.
479 Lyn: Mm-hmm
480 Don: And I think boy that's somethin to be it's somethin t'be respected
481   if not liked, y'know what he does with it I think um
482 Lyn: It's kinda like can you blame somebody when they do something
483   wrong but they don't know they're don't know they're doin
484   it wrong?
485 Don: (3 sec)   Yeah I mean he's I mean he's just..he's acting on uh
486   ya know he's acting on this on on with such forcefulness (2 sec)
487   I dunno y'know I mean there's something, well there's hesitation

488		about it um..n that's (2 sec) ⌈y'know.
489	Lyn:	⌊He doesn't have a conscience at that
490		point.
491	Don:	Yes /?/
492	Lyn:	If he doesn't have a conscience can can you blame im can you be
493		really angry with im?
494	Don:	(3 sec) No no ya really can't (5 sec) /Nobody/ really can't (3 sec)
495		blame Alex.

The talk moves on to the conventions of movies and movie endings.

520	Lyn:	But in the movie when you go to the cinema an if everything
521		ends up happily ever after, things don't always work out, okay?
522	Don:	Well no an an y'know n that's why I uh (2 sec) that's why I find
523		then sometin like "Pretty Woman" or "Officer and a Gentleman"
524		or you know this this
525	Lyn:	/??/ Those those are different different stories though. Those
526		are love movies. (2 sec) This isn't a love story (little laugh)
527	Don:	(3 sec) Yeah but I mean that that that there's a there's a there's a
528		certain..unrealistic and and and..and I--
529	Lyn:	But they are fairytales.
530	Don:	They are they're fairy tales, um
531	Lyn:	Why are they fairy tales? Cinderella (4 sec) (laughs)
532	Don:	I'm sorry I'm just not big on Cinderella stories (Lyn laughs)I I
533		just I dunno I think I just have this darker vision of things⌈/ ? /
534	Lyn:	⌊I love
535		Cinderella stories.

Don explains at this point in a lengthy turn how predictable "Cinderella" stories are and why he objects to them. Then he resumes the "conference" and asks Lyn if she has other papers to discuss.

For a total of 136 turns, Don and Lyn actually converse, sharing in the development and initiation of topics, agreeing and disagreeing, interrupting each other to elaborate on their partner's previous comment, talking over one another to follow through a thread and then returning to shared topics. Lyn's sudden shift from conference to conversation takes Don by surprise. But, like Mary, he accepts Lyn's offer of a different relationship. Between the two of them, they construct an analysis of the book and the movie, talking about lack of connections between scenes, reader and viewer response, foreshadowing, and control. They move then into an even larger context, to the topic introduced by Lyn—paradigmatic structure for movies. Here, Lyn offers some disagreement with Don, but unlike disagreement in other conferences, because of the shared perspective and the inclusive positions they've adopted, it remains simple disagreement, not challenge. Talk is almost symmetrical during this segment, a highly atypical teaching situation but one in which Lyn demonstrated on her own terms what she knew and how she felt, and had the opportunity to place those responses and that knowledge in a context other than the usual classroom one. She constructed the opportunity to imagine a larger audience than her teacher.

Rick and Lyn, in conjunction with willing teachers, were able to shift the traditional student-teacher relationship. There is a real change in the tone and pattern of speech; transcribing these tapes, I immediately heard that shift, heard a new intensity. Rick is excited, and he shares his story with enthusiasm, while Mary laughs freely, gasping at some information and asking questions that show her involvement. Lyn and Don joust after Lyn's evaluation of the book. These teachers and students share information and ideas, and learning is taking place in ways that hold promise for a fundamental change in a power structure that has resisted that change. What would happen if students learned to challenge assumptions? To offer a conversational gambit? To answer questions with questions? To draw attention to power structures and challenge them?

What Students Want From Conferences: Envisioning a New Relationship

At my request, colleagues have asked their students to write about their best and worst conferences and to describe or define what a conference is or does or should be. Many of these conference descriptions indicate that students are aware of and resent the kind of control that so discouraged me as I analyzed the transcripts of my research conferences. They feel keenly the anger that accompanies being silenced, the frustration of being dominated and confused.

> In my [first-year composition] class last semester my teacher had conferences with everyone in the class. I remember thinking, "Great, just another half hour that I have to come in and spend with a person I don't want to talk to." But I realized that this conference could be valuable to me. My teacher wasn't going to talk the entire time; I would have a chance to voice

my opinion also. I walked into her office with an open mind, ready to get something accomplished. But to my surprise, the teacher dominated the conference. When I finally had a chance to speak, she closed her mind. Completely unreasonable, my teacher would not budge an inch. She had completely closed her mind to the situation. Nothing new was accomplished, and I look at this conference as a failure.

Another student describes a conference that started off well but wound up being a frustrating experience.

The teacher was very kind and she was giving me ideas, but then the paper started turning into her paper rather than mine. By the time the session was over I felt as if I had to return home and try and express my teacher's ideas in my paper to give what she wanted. In the end, my paper took forever to do, it was a mess, and I hated it.

There are two strands that run through the responses. One strand is affective: students are afraid, nervous, excited, or uncertain of themselves and want to talk about those feelings, want to talk about those feelings, want some reassurance. I've written about this in chapter five; here, I simply want to say that when students ask that teachers acknowledge their feelings, I am reminded of Giroux's assertion of the need for us to remember that students' "drives, emotions, and interests" provide momentum for learning itself" (107). The second strand indicates that students perceive conferences as goal-oriented: teachers and students meet in their institutional capacities to discuss a problem with a paper. Repeatedly, students write that they want "guidance," to be set on the "right track," they want "to accomplish" something, they want a writing problem "solved." They want the teacher to draw on his or her expertise in the field and apply it to the problem the student wants assistance with. Comments should be "clear" and "constructive," not just critical. "Conferences are a time for individuals (usually professor and student) to come together and rediscover original objectives. This often entails review of past work and discussion of a new or continued direction. Conferences help clear up questions and get everybody on the same page."

Students demand that teachers acknowledge their authority. What does the teacher know that can help the student? This is not the unambiguous request, "What will it take to get an A?" (One reason I think this question makes teachers cringe is that it baldly acknowledges what we so often try to pretend isn't so—that *we* have the authority to set standards, that an "A" is what we say it is.) Rather, the student here articulates with a metaphor what runs through many responses: the student and teacher need to be on the same page, but not necessarily reading it the same way.

Just as it is students who disrupt the ordinary patterns of power and knowledge in the conferences I've studied, it is students who envision a new relationship with their teachers. One of the students above calls for mutual learning in the conference, for "rediscovery" of the original objectives. He is asking that objectives be excavated from all that has buried them over the semester; he is suggesting that reflection is part of discovery and is a necessary component of conferencing. Another student concludes his discussion of conferencing by describing a relationship between teacher and student that is mutually responsive, active, supportive, and symmetrical: "I think a conference is a place where both people learn about each other, their ideas and experiences, and relate to each other their ideas to help one another grow." The concept of the teacher learning from the student and using that learning in an even wider community is echoed in the description one woman provided of a conference she enjoyed with her systems analysis professor. She writes: "To me, conferences should be times when a teacher and student learn from each other; the teacher learns how he/she can help the student (possibly enabling the teacher to better understand how to help others) and the student should learn from the teacher (how to solve their particular problems)."

I learn from students when I forget that I am a teacher. I learn from them when the traditional hierarchies have been disrupted and suddenly the two of us have access to the same information, are involved together in the process of creating knowledge. One of the foundational tenets of critical pedagogy is that the teacher must also be a learner. It is difficult to learn when we are engaged not in dialogue with our students and the larger communities we all represent, but in a monologue delivered in a cocoon. The student who asked for comments that weren't all critical but constructive is asking for the language of possibility to be used when we meet and talk. Once we understand what is not effective, not "working" and why, how can we re-envision it? What are the possibilities for a paper? For a relationship? How can writing this paper, approaching this material, sharing my thoughts with other students and my family and the communities of which I am a part help to empower me or others?

How can I effect change? Students want conferences to live up to their possibilities. Their responses are full of the language of hope—and the angry language of smashed hopes.

Demystifying Conferences, Sharing Power

Both students and teachers agree that while successful conferences may involve teaching, they always involve learning of some sort, and in the best conferences, there is active, mutual learning. What I've seen in the study conferences is that passive learning is the norm and opportunities for active learning are rare, requiring the cooperation of both teacher and student. But creating those opportunities requires that both participants more fully understand conferencing as a genre of speech, something that has conventions and that those conventions can be tossed aside or clung to, depending upon what each person desires or has the knowledge and power to demand. We need to be trained in the genre as do our students. Most of these conferences were requested by the teacher, and while teachers conference with many different students, possibly gaining a greater repertoire of conferencing techniques (I say "possibly" because the conferences I've listened to don't indicate that the teacher individualizes conferencing to the extent that we would like to believe), students conference less frequently and with fewer teachers. Some students who responded to my questions about the nature of conferencing indicated that they had little or no experience to draw on. For such students, conferencing is a vague and abstract concept, but one they will perhaps learn more about—unfortunately sometimes from teachers with no training or critical reflection.

If we think about how we might teach our students about poetry—and how we've learned and continue to learn about poetry ourselves—we can begin to reconstruct our notions about writing conferences. What counts as a poem? When does a poem push the limits? Prose poems? Found poetry created from words seen in a subway station? Ten word poems? Is it a conference if we don't discuss a single word of text? How long or short can a conference be? Some of us learned that a poem is rhymed and has a distinctive shape on a page and are stunned to read prose poems and disconcerted to read poems that play with the language of a repair manual. When I asked colleagues for conference tapes, one sent a set of tapes that comprised one two-hour conference held over two days. The student and teacher wound their way through topics that clearly connected to the text as well as many that were far more personal. He insisted that this was normal for him. Another gave me several conference tapes that included meetings with writing groups of three students, a typical practice for her. In her tapes, students sometimes held brief "side-conversations" as she spoke with just one student, then all four would speak about a single topic. Like prose poems and found poetry, these pushed against the edges of what I understood to be most common, and so I began my work with the one-to-one conferences. What is clear, though, is that as a genre, conferences—like poems—can come in many forms.

We need to consider not just structure, but purpose—why it is that we conference. If it is to "get to know" our students, to hear their experiences, is there a reason why we might want to hear them privately, rather than have them share those experiences with their classmates? If students share their experiences with each other, in class, won't they begin to build a community, to change each other's lives in subtle ways? What is the benefit of sharing only with me? And if I am encouraging critical reflection, if many voices can better make a student rethink or understand her experiences in new ways, why should my voice be the only one she hears or thinks "counts?" If I am going to be critical and reflective about my own practice, I have to ask myself: What do I want to know? Why do I want to know that? What do I want students to know about me? When would I tell them something privately? Do I forsee myself saying the same thing over and over with each student? If so, is our time better served by my telling them all at once, in class interview? How will I use what I learn from my students? Will I use that information to change resistance into submission, to draw students into an academic structure as easily as possible? Or do I want to know so that I can begin to learn what strengths, what values, what lives and constructions my students bring with them individually as a way to initially structure a class and develop community?

Rather than initial "get to know you" conferences, each of us constructs an introductory portfolio and shares it during the first week or so in class. We each select three items of importance to us and provide initially a brief written introduction to those pieces. We share them first in a small group, where the stories that give those items meaning are swapped, then select one of the three items to share with the whole class, again telling the story, this time in a way that has been shaped by the telling a few minutes earlier, when we learned what most interested classmates, what information was needed or wanted. I read all the written introductions and respond personally, not institutionally—no grade. When I return the introductions and students comment about the lack of a grade, we can begin talking about power, about expectations, about active and passive learning.

I ask students to read the syllabus and to work in small groups to generate questions about the class and about me; I acknowledge that I am at the moment a focus of attention and curiosity and talk with them about why this is so. I also let them know that I am intensely curious about them, their experiences and beliefs and goals. In this way, we begin immediately exploring the traditional power structure of the class. We do a whole-class conference at that point. My openness in answering questions, my willingness to tell and listen to stories—not just lecture—help develop a relationship of trust. As I do so, my language shifts back and forth: I cannot speak of my father without my eastern working-poor dialect and without incorporating the kind of sly humor I admire in him. As I move between academic and home languages, I model for students a way of coexisting in these two worlds.

Students are acutely aware of the ways in which some questions elicit surface information and others delve more deeply, and after we have answered questions about each other, we talk about how questions are structured and how they work to change or support the usual teacher-student relationship. We talk about the ways each of us has shaped the conference, and move from there to talking about conferencing. Here, I ask them to describe their worst or best conferences and to tell me what conferences should do, what they should feel like. In small and large groups, we compare responses and begin to construct some goals for conferencing, to explore what is possible, what is desirable. We begin to see that there doesn't have to be one single, simple model for how that talk might be shaped.

As I worked through my research, I asked myself questions about the value of conferencing. I began to feel as if I was making an argument that conferencing is not nearly as important as we would like to believe and that perhaps we shouldn't conference. Nonetheless, I always had the "felt sense" that conferencing was important, was necessary. Critical educators are concerned with the use of "emancipatory authority," that is, the use of authority and power for social change—the empowerment of oppressed groups, the end of exploitive practices, the elimination of systemic inequality. Conferences don't usually "just happen"—somebody requests or demands one. Given a choice, my guess is that students would prefer to schedule conferences only when they want them, which might be rare in non-empowering classrooms; teachers often require conferences because they think the student needs it whether the student thinks so or not. As reflective, critical teachers, we have to ask ourselves whether we will use our power to schedule conferences, and if so, why.

I schedule conferences initially for several reasons. In some ways, for me, it is part of pedagogical pluralism. I neither learn in just one way nor teach in one fashion, but am constantly adapting to my students, to the contexts we are creating together, and to changing goals. Further, critical practitioners like Giroux and McLaren point out the importance of the teacher in using power to help students learn to analyze their experiences, to place them in different social contexts, and to learn a discourse that allows for critique and possibility. While the opportunity and maybe even the temptation to misuse power in a conference may be enormous, the opportunity for transformation is also enormous. I have written earlier about the ways in which the conversational aspects of conferencing often encourage students to share personal experiences and teachers who see themselves as speaking partners are prompted to share as well. The intimacy of that setting, of that exchange, is transformative. We cannot go back easily to a traditional institutional relationship. I can also see the argument for requiring conferences in order to provide students with experience in a speech genre so closely connected to power, access to information, and the discourse of the community students are attempting to join or have been required to be a part of.

I can, however, understand not requiring students to participate in conferences, for the negotiation of authority and control is an integral part of learning. After a couple of conferences, I leave it up to the individual student to schedule conferences with me, unless I have a specific reason to speak with the student privately. But if conferences are seen as part of the whole experience of learning and students feel empowered and responsible, most continue to schedule conferences.

How do conferences "count" in my curriculum? Although at one time I ignored that issue, assuming that I only counted conferences as part of participation, critical discourse analysis has forced me to rethink the ways in which I am evaluating my students. In the learning community my students and I envision, dividing a course grade into smaller units becomes more difficult—there is less emphasis on discrete skills. If my goal is to teach students to question their experiences and to restructure knowledge in ways that are connected to a democratic ethic, then I need to think carefully about the ways in which students can demonstrate their thinking and learning in a one-to-one situation. I need to be conscious of ways in which I construct talk which might not encourage that demonstration. Any system of evaluation rests on values, and should be established after discussion about what the various communities represented by the teacher and students find most important.

I also need to think carefully about how my students can evaluate me, can help me learn at the same time they're learning. When I last conferenced, I had just begun the process of asking students to share a partially guided evaluation of their conferences with me as a way of checking to make sure we were "on the same page" so to speak. I also wrote an evaluation for the student. The guiding questions included "What was the most helpful comment (if any) that I gave you? What did you enjoy most? Were there times when you were lost, confused, angry, frustrated or surprised, or particularly pleased? Please provide me with as much detail as you can about these moments. What can I do in the future to help construct a better conference? What can you do? Do we need to set up another conference?" I responded in a similar way to my students, and we exchanged these the next class meeting after the conference.

I think this kind of reflective and analytical practice is helpful in teaching students to be critical and hopeful. A conference provides a shared experience between teacher and student, a sliver of common knowledge. Collaborating to analyze and transform this experience, learning to use it to effect change, is an extension of critical pedagogy in the classroom.

Just as critical pedagogy insists upon exposing any hidden agenda in the classroom or elsewhere, there should be no hidden agenda for a conference. If I have asked a student to conference with me, I should tell him or her as clearly as I can why. What issues do I want to raise and why? What texts or experiences do I want to discuss? What can the student reasonably expect to happen when we meet? What should she or he bring to help us confer? Some of these suggestions seem simple, even trivial. But I remember conferences with teachers where I worked myself into a frenzy of anxiety and self-doubt before I walked into the office because I didn't know what I'd done wrong, where I'd failed. I didn't bring papers, poems, textbooks, or some material with me that was necessary to the conference. In not doing so, I "failed" all over again—I wasn't prepared, I hadn't anticipated my teacher's needs, I wasn't a good student. Sharing an agenda in advance is part of showing your hand, giving up the power to surprise and control. It the beginning of a more equal relationship, one based on learning and not gatekeeping, on changing relations, not maintaining the status quo.

It seems to me that it's not only me who needs to rethink conferencing as a standard, ordinary, unquestioned practice, but the whole discipline of composition, which has been one of its most vociferous supporters. We have to examine what it is we want from conferencing and we have to explore the possibility that it often doesn't accomplish those things—it just doesn't work. So far, conferencing practice seems to have escaped the net of "accountability" that has caught up the rest of the academic world, and we continue with a practice that is cherished but unexamined. If we are critically reflective about the ways in which we are constructing and reproducing harmful concepts and structures, then we will be learners with our students. We will be modeling the ways in which our experiences matter, the ways in which we can use them to transform society. If a critical analysis of conferencing has shown that it is something less than we had hoped, that it fails in many ways to achieve what we wanted it to, then we can still go back to the hope while interrogating the practice.

Dana was fishing for help when she gathered up the courage to ask Eric how to be insightful. And each time we talk with each other about conferences, we are fishing in murky waters, hoping for answers. But when we fish with our words, we are fishing together, students and teachers, weaving a net, writing that long story.

WORKS CITED

Bakhtin, M.M. 1986. *Speech genres and other late essays.* Trans. V.W. McGee. Ed. C. Emerson and M. Holquist. Austin: U. Texas P.

Banks, J. A. 1981. *Education in the 80's: Multiethnic education.* Washington, D.C.: National Education Association.

Belenkey, M.F., Clinchy, B.M., Goldberger, N.R., and Tarule, J.M. 1986. *Women's ways of knowing: The development of self, voice, and mind.* New York: Basic Books.

Black, L., D.A. Daiker, J. Sommers, and G. Stygall. 1994. *New directions in portfolio assessment: Reflective practice, critical theory, and large-scale scoring.* Portsmouth, NH: Heinemann/Boynton-Cook.

Black, L. 1992. "Observing English 101: Gender and knowledge in an adult composition classroom. Paper presented at the Conference on College Composition and Communication, March, Boston.

Bruch, P. and Marback, R. 1997. Race identity, writing, and the politics of dignity: Reinvigorating the ethics of "Students' right to their own language." *Journal of Advanced Composition,* 17.2: 267-281.

Bruffee, K. A. 1986. Social construction, language, and the authority of knowledge: A bibliographic essay. *College English,* 48.8: 773-790.

Bruffee, K.A. 1985. *A short course in writing.* Boston: Little.

Butler, J. 1992. *Gender trouble: Feminism and the subversion of identity.* New York: Routledge & Kegan Paul.

Campbell, K. E. 1997. "Real niggaz's don't die": African American students speaking themselves into their writing. In C. Severino, et al.: 67-78.

Carnicelli, T. 1985. The writing conference: A one-to-one conversation. In T. Donovan and B. McClelland, eds., *Eight approaches to teaching composition,* 101-131. Urbana, IL: NCTE.

Chodorow, N. 1978. *The reproduction of mothering.* Berkeley: University of California P.

Connor, U. 1997. Contrastive rhetoric: Implications for teachers of writing in multicultural classrooms. In C. Severino, et al.: 198-208.

Delpit, L.D. 1988. The silenced dialogue: Power and pedagogy in educating other people's children. *Harvard Educational Review,* 58.3: 280-298.

Duke, C. 1975. The student-centered conference and the writing process. *English Journal*, 64: 44-78.

Fairclough, N. 1993. Critical discourse analysis and the marketization of public discourse: The universities. *Discourse and Society*, 4.2: 133-168.

Feehan, M. 1989. Conferencing, culture, and common sense. *Freshman English News*, 17.2: 17- 19.

Fiksdale, S. 1990. *The right time and pace: A microanalysis of cross-cultural gate-keeping interviews.* Norwood, NJ: Ablex.

Fishman, P.M. 1978. What do couples talk about when they're alone? In D. Butturff and E. Epstein, eds., *Women's language and style*, 11-22. Akron, OH: Dept. of English, University of Akron.

Foster, M. 1995. Talking that talk: The language of control, curriculum, and critique. *Linguistics and Education* 7.2: 129-150.

Freedman, S. and A. Katz. 1987. Pedagogical interaction during the composing process: The writing conference. In A. Matsuhashi ed., *Writing in real time: Modeling production processes*, 58-80. Norwood, NJ: Ablex.

Freedman, S. and M. Sperling. 1985. Written language acquistion: The role of response and the writing conference. In S. Freedman, ed., *The acquisition of written language*, 106-130. Norwood, NJ: Ablex.

Garrison, R. 1974. One-to-one: Tutorial instruction for freshman composition. In R. Garrison, ed., *New directions for community colleges: Implementing innovative instruction*, 54-83. San Francisco: Jossey-Bass.

Gilligan, C. 1982. *In a different voice: Psychological theory and women's development.* Cambridge, MA: Harvard UP.

Giroux, H.A. 1988. *Schooling and the struggle for public life: Critical pedagogy in the modern age.* Minneapolis: University of Minneapolis Press.

Grijalva, M. 1997. Teaching American Indian students: Interpreting the rhetorics of silence. In C. Severino, et al.: 40-50.

Harris, M. 1997. Cultural conflicts in the writing center: Expectations and assumptions of ESL students. In C. Severino, et al.: 220-233.

Heath, S.B. 1983. *Ways with words: Language, life, and work in communities and classrooms.* London: Cambridge UP.

Herman, E.S. and N. Chomsky. 1988. *Manufacturing consent: The political economy of the mass media.* New York: Pantheon Books.

Hiatt, M.P. 1975. Students at bay: The myth of the conference. *College Composition and Communication*, 26: 38-41.

hooks, b. 1994. *Teaching to transgress: Education as the practice of freedom.* NY: Routledge & Kegan Paul.

———. 1989. *Talking back: Thinking feminist, thinking black.* Boston: South End Press.

Howard, R. M. 1996. The great wall of African American vernacular English in the American college classroom. *Journal of Advanced Composition*, 16.2: 265-284.

Jacobs, S.E. and A.B. Karliner. 1977. Helping writers to think: The effect of speech roles in individual conferences on the quality of thought in student writing. *College English*, 38.5: 489- 505.

Jamieson, S. 1997. Composition readers and the construction of identity. In C. Severino, et al.: 150-171.

Knapp, J.V. 1976. Contract/conference evaluations of freshman composition. *College English*, 37.7: 647-653.

Labov, W. 1972. *Language in the inner city: Studies in the black English vernacular*. Philadelphia: University of Pennsylvania Press.

Labov. W. and D. Fanshel. 1977. *Therapeutic discourse*. New York: Academic Press.

Lakoff, R. 1975. *Language and women's place*. New York: Harper.

Lisle, B. and Mano, S. 1997. Embracing a multicultural rhetoric. In C. Severino:12-26.

McClaren, P. 1989. *Life in schools: An introduction to critical pedagogy in the foundations of education*. New York: Longman.

Mortenson, P.L. 1992. Analyzing talk about writing. In G. Kirsh and P. Sullivan, eds., *Methods and methodology in composition research*, 105-129. Carbondale: Southern Illinois UP.

Murray, D.M. 1985. *A writer teaches writing*. Boston: Houghton Mifflin.

Murray, D.M. 1979. The listening eye: Reflections on the writing conference. *College English*, 41.1: 13-18.

Newkirk, T. 1989. The first five minutes: Setting the agenda in a writing conference. In C. Anson, ed., *Writing and response: Theory, practice, and research*, 317-331. Urbana, IL: NCTE.

O'Barr, W.M. and B.K. Atkins. 1980. Women's language or powerless language? In S. McConnell-Ginet, R. Borker, and N. Furman, eds., *Women and language in literature and society*, 92-110. New York: Praeger.

Okawa, G.Y. 1997. Cross-talk: Talking cross-difference. In C. Severino, et al.: 94-102.

Rist, R.C. 1970. Student social class and teacher expectations: The self-fulfilling prophecy in ghetto education. *Harvard Educational Review*, 40.3: 411-451.

Rose, A. 1982. Spoken versus written criticism of student writing: Some advantages of the conference method. *College Composition and Communication*, 33: 326-330.

Sacks, H., E. Schlegoff, and G. Jefferson. 1974. A simplest systematic for the organization of turn taking for conversation. *Language*, 50: 696-735.

Sadker, M. and D. Sadker. 1986. Sexism in the classroom: From grade school to graduate school. *Phi Delta Kappan*, 67.7: 512-515.

Sadker, M. and D. Sadker. 1984. Year III: Final report, promoting effectiveness in classroom instruction. Washington, D.C.: NIE Contract No. 400-80-0033.

Severino, C., J.C. Guerra, and J.E. Butler, eds. 1997. *Writing in multicultural settings*. New York: MLA.

Shaughnessy, M. 1977. *Errors and expectations*. New York: Oxford UP.

Shiffrin, D. 1988. *Discourse Markers*. NY: Cambridge UP.

Silva, T. 1997. Differences in ESL and native-English-speaker writing: The research and its implications. In C. Severino, et al.: 209-219.

Simkins-Bullock, J.A. and B.G. Wildman. 1991. An investigation into the relationship between gender and language. *Sex Roles*, 24: 149-160.

Sinclair, J. McH. And M. Coulthard. 1975. *Towards an analysis of discourse.* London: Oxford UP.

Smitherman, G. 1986. *Talkin and testifyin: The language of Black America.* Detroit: Wayne State UP.

Spender, D. 1989. *The writing or the sex?, or why you don't have to read women's writing to know it's no good.* New York: Pergamon.

Sperling, M. 1990. I want to talk to each of you: Collaboration and the teacher-student writing conference. *Research in the Teaching of English,* 24.3: 279-321.

Squire, J.R. and R.K. Applebee. 1968. *High school English instruction today: The national student of high school English programs.* New York: Appleton-Century-Crofts.

Stanback, M.H. 1985. Language and black woman's place: Evidence from the black middle class. In P. Treichler and C. Kramerae, eds., *For Alma Mater.* Chicago: U. Illinois.

Stubbs, M. 1983. *Discourse analysis: The sociolinguistic analysis of natural language.* Chicago: U. Chicago P.

Stygall, G. 1998. Compromised positionings: Women and language in the Collaborative Writing Classroom. In S. Jarratt and L. Worsham, eds., *In other words: Feminism and composition,* 318- 341. New York: MLA.

Swann, J. 1988. Talk control: An illustration from the classroom of problems in analysing male dominance of conversation. In J. Coates and J. Cameron, eds., *Women in their speech communities,* 123-140. New York: Longman.

Tannen, D. 1982. Ethnic style in male-female conversation. In J.J. Gumperz, ed., *Language and social identity* 217-231. New York: Cambridge UP.

Tharp, R.G., S. Dalton, and L.Yamauchi 1994. Principles for culturally compatible Native American education. *Journal of Navajo Education,* 11.3, 33-39.

Tobin, L. 1990. Productive tension in the writing conference: Studying our students and ourselves. In T. Newkirk, ed., *To compose: Teaching writing in high school and college,* 95-112. Portsmouth, NH: Heinemann.

Troutman, D. 1997. Whose voice is it anyway? Marked features in the writing of Black English speakers. In C. Severino, et al.: 27-39.

Ulichney, P. and K.W. Watson-Gegeo. 1989. Interactions and authority: The dominant framework in writing conferences. *Discourse Processes,* 12: 309-328.

van Dijk, T. 1993. Principles of critical discourse analysis. *Discourse and Society,* 4.2: 249-283.

Villa, J. 1996. "To soar like the eagle": An empowering freshman composition class for American Indian students. Unpublished dissertation. University of New Mexico.

Villanueva, V. 1993. *Bootstraps: From an American academic of color.* Urbana, IL: NCTE.

Walker, C.P. and D. Elias. 1987. Writing conference talk: Factors associated with high- and low-rated writing conferences. *Research in the Teaching of English,* 21.3: 266-285.

Witte, S., P. Meyer, T. Miller, and L. Faigley. 1982. *A national survey of college and university program directors Tech. Rep. No. 2.* Austin, TX: The University of Texas, Writing Assessment Project.

Wong, I.B. 1988. Teacher-student talk in technical writing conferences. *Written Communication,* 5.4.: 444-460.

APPENDIX A

Teacher-Student Conference Pairs

Male Teacher/Male Student

    Bill / Mike
    Carl / Dave
    Eric / Ben

Female Teacher/Female Student

    Erin / Leah
    Mary / Gail
    Nina / Kate
    Nina / Lily

Male Teacher/Female Student

    Bill / Cari
    Don /Eva
    Don / Lyn
    Eric / Dana

Female Teacher/Male Student

    Erin /Jeff
    Mary / Rick
    Nina / John

APPENDIX B

Transcription Notations

[	=	overlapping speech
⌊	=	no gap in speech between speakers
CAPS	=	stressed word
--	=	interruption
-	=	sudden cessation of speech with a glottal stop
..	=	half second pause; each additional half-second is indicated by one additional period
()	=	parentheses enclose commentary by transcriber
//	=	words enclosed by slashes are difficult to understand on the tape and may be inaccurately transcribed
italics	=	reference to a word as a word. Example: "The second *and* in this sentence is not necessary."

APPENDIX C

Word Count

Conference Pair	Total # of Words	Teacher # / % of Total	Student# / % of Total
Nina / Lily	1922	1877 / 97.6	45 / 2.3
Eric / Ben	4285	4009 / 93.4	273 / 6.3
Nina / Kate	2881	2591 / 89.9	290 / 10.1
Erin / Leah	4070	3195 / 86.8	536 / 13.1
Erin / Jeff	3586	3052 / 85.0	534 / 14.8
Nina / John	2386	2022 / 84.6	364 / 15.2
Carl / Dave	2307	1936 / 83.8	371 / 16.2
Bill / Cari	3439	2761 / 80.2	678 / 19.7
Don / Eva	4439	3345 / 75.2	1094 / 24.6
Don / Lyn	5347	4043 / 74.3	1324 / 25.2
Eric / Dana	6739	4822 / 71.4	1917 / 28.4
Mary / Gail	3682	2605 / 70.6	1077 / 29.2
Bill / Mike	2965	1844 / 62.1	1121 / 37.8
Mary / Rick	3428	2045 / 59.6	1383 / 40.2

Percentage of Word Count by Gender Sets

Male Teacher / Male Student		*Female Teacher / Male Student*	
Bill 62.1	Mike 37.8	Erin 85.0	Jeff 14.8
Eric 93.4	Ben 6.3	Nina 84.6	John 15.2
Carl 83.8	Dave 16.2	Mary 59.6	Rick 40.2
Average 79.7%	20.1%	76.4%	23.4%

Male Teacher / Female Student		*Female Teacher / Female Student*	
Bill 80.2	Cari 19.7	Erin 86.8	Leah 13.1
Don 75.2	Eva 24.6	Nina 89.9	Kate 10.1
Don 74.3	Lyn 25.2	Nina 97.6	Lily 2.3
Eric 71.4	Dana 28.4	Mary 59.6	Gail 29.2
Average 75.2%	24.4%	86.2%	13.6%

APPENDIX D

Discourse Markers

Dyad	*And*	*So*	*Well*	*But*	*You Know*	*I Mean*
Erin/Jeff	6/10	19/5	8/3	15/4	20/10	5/2
Nina/John	40/11	11/2	8/3	11/2	28/4	7/0
Mary/Rick	20/26	17/26	13/2	10/9	3/13	4/2
Total	126/47	47/33	29/8	36/15	51/27	16/4
Carl/Dave	43/8	9/0	5/1	10/1	2/1	3/0
Eric/Ben	47/2	20/5	7/0	25/0	13/6	33/1
Bill/Mike	31/17	10/4	2/5	20/6	9/15	6/3
Total	121/27	39/9	14/6	55/7	24/22	32/4
Erin/Leah	61/11	17/1	9/1	9/7	5/1	0/3
Mary/Gail	52/13	17/8	11/3	27/8	10/12	15/5
Nina/Kate	38/1	12/2	4/0	26/2	53/2	11/3
Nina/Lily	48/0	8/0	3/0	11/0	33/0	0/0
Total	199/25	54/11	27/4	73/17	101/15	27/11
Bill/Cari	57/7	14/3	3/0	7/6	8/0	5/1
Don/Eva	84/18	7/7	21/1	14/6	84/4	19/5
Don/Lyn	107/33	20/2	46/6	29/11	130/2	54/2
Eric/Dana	77/47	23/5	21/3	32/11	24/13	77/37
Total	325/105	54/17	91/10	32/11	246/19	155/45

Discourse Markers by Gender and Role

And
Used by female teachers=325
Used by male teachers=446
Used by female students=130 With=524
Used by male students=74 With=247

But
Used by female teachers=109
Used by male teachers=147
Used by female students=51 With=165
Used by male students=22 With=91

So
Used by female teachers=101
Used by male teachers=147
Used by female students=28 With=118
Used by male students=41 With=86

You Know
Used by female teachers=152
Used by male teachers=270
Used by female students=34 With=347
Used by male students=49 With=75

Well
Used by female teachers=56
Used by male teachers=105
Used by female students=14 With=118
Used by male students=14 With=43

I Mean
Used by female teachers=43
Used by male teachers=197
Used by female students=56 With=182
Used by male students=8 With=58

ABOUT THE AUTHOR

LAUREL JOHNSON BLACK IS AN ASSISTANT PROFESSOR OF ENGLISH AT Indiana University of Pennsylvania, where she teaches courses in writing, literature, and sociolinguistics. She has an M.F.A. in poetry from the University of Iowa and a Ph.D. in composition from Miami University of Ohio. She has published essays and articles on portfolios, classroom practice, and her own working class background. She is interested in issues of language and culture from kitchens to classrooms, fleamarkets to boardrooms.

DATE DUE

FEB 0 8 2002			
FEB 0 8 2003			
GAYLORD			PRINTED IN U.S.A